THE GREAT MYSTERY OF LIFE BEYOND DEATH

The idea of survival after death compels every courageous mind to scrutinise the evidence and dissect the hidden elements surrounding death and lay bare the core truth.

The varied experiences which a spirit undergoes after death are described in this book with clarity and verisimilitude, giving the reader a rare glimpse of another, unknown dimension. Regardless of its provenance, the book makes fascinating reading and will certainly provide food for thought, even for the most hardened sceptic.

THE GREAT MYSTERY
OF
LIFE BEYOND DEATH

PROF. HIRALAL L. KAJI,
I.E.S. (Retd.)

Foreword by
V.R. KRISHNA IYER
Former Judge, Supreme Court of India

New Age Books

ISBN: 978-81-7822-138-0

Reprint: Delhi, 2009

Second Revised Edition: Delhi, 2003

Published by
NEW AGE BOOKS
A-44 Naraina Phase-I
New Delhi-110 028 (INDIA)
Email: nab@vsnl.in
Website: www.newagebooksindia.com

Printed in India
at Shri Jainendra Press
A-45 Naraina Phase-I, New Delhi-110 028

"I can assure the readers that this is the genuine work of Sir Arthur Conan Doyle and that it is a nearly correct exposition of the most mysterious secret of human life."

Shree Yama Raj

FOREWORD

"I am a wayfarer of an endless road.
My greetings of a wanderer to thee."
—*Rabindranath Tagore*

Immortality, an inalienable attribute of every *atman,* invests the grosser phenomena of birth and death with a compulsive mystery to explore and conquer —an activity which belongs to the domain of scientific inquiry. The laws of material phenomena and the critical investigation of spiritual nature are viewed in anti-thesis by superstitious scientific cowards who dare not travel beyond the grosser sensory perceptions, measurements and experiences, but are envisioned as a super-synthesis by the enlightened truth-seekers for whom the occult is a challenge for fascinating entry into the unknown areas of cosmic law and order and break-down of the barrier between matter and spirit and a shift from blinkered views to broader vistas. Science has no monopoly of absolute truths and sages have woven Nature and Supernature into Reality in its totality. That is why that American agnostic humanist, Robert Ingersoll observed:

"Every cradle asks us whence;
every coffin whither !"

Tagore in one of his final songs of the *Gitanjali*, welcomes death *not* as an inevitable evil but as a delectable fulfilment:

"O Thou the last fulfilment of life, Death,
My death, come and whisper to me !"

All this may sound strange but 'the most beautiful experience we can have is the mysterious' (Albert Einstein).

Socrates said with inspired wisdom and fearless truth:

> "To fear death, gentlemen, is nothing other than to think oneself wise when one is not; for it is to think one knows what one does not know. No man knows whether death may not even turn out to be the greatest of blessings for a human being; and yet people fear it as if they knew for certain that it is the greatest of evils."

Indian seers and legends have affirmed that death is not the end of the road but a bend in the journey, that it is not a wall but a door, that Nachiketa and Savitri are not poetic fancy or flights of futility but super-reality. Psychic breakthrough, with the master-key of higher faculties, is authentic, if validated by scientific veracity.

True, survival after death as an assertive bigotry based on lore and myth, is goofy gullibility, wasted vanity and scriptural ignorance. But subtle explorations, astral experiments, trans-corporeal phenomena, fool-proof materialisation and factual proof beyond reasonable doubt inexplicable except on the basis of transmortal life, subtle in form but verifiable like any other material verity, compel every courageous mind, freed from the fanaticism of materialism to scrutinise the evidence and dissect the hidden elements surrounding death and lay bare the core truth freed from the muddy creed.

Life and Death have now been subjected to investigation from the scientific perspective and the emerging factual finding is that to shuffle off one's mortal coil does not reduce Life to nothingness but inaugurates a viable, wonderful incorporeal survival governed by laws of postmortem existence, with capability for communication with the living and even occasional materialisation. All this is supported by escalating earthly testimony beyond imaginative projections, happy hallucinations and dreamy fantasies.

What I should drive home before I go beyond is the need to adapt the method of science to any problem including the question of survival after death which, please note, is not other worldliness but this-worldliness on a different non-physical dimension, subtle, yet real, occult—but not cult. Claude Bernard has rightly stressed:

> ". . . .in nature what is absurd, according to our theories, is not always impossible.
>
> . . . .facts. . . .exist which mean nothing to most minds while they are full of light for others. It even happens that a fact or observation stays a very long time under the eyes of a man of science without in any way inspiring him; then suddenly there comes a ray of light, and the mind interprets the fact quite differently and finds for it wholly new relations. The new idea appears. . .as a kind of sudden revelation. . .The experimental method, then cannot give new and fruitful ideas to men who have none; it can serve only to guide the ideas of men who have them, to direct their ideas and to develop them so as to get the best results.
>
> "The idea is a seed; the (experimental) method is the earth furnishing the conditions in which it may develop, flourish and give the best of fruit according to its nature. But as only what has been sown in the ground will ever grow in it, so nothing will be developed by the experimental method except the ideas submitted to it. The method itself gives birth to nothing."

It may be apt to begin 'Beyond Death' with a quote from Lyall Watson:

> "The most interesting evidence ever gathered in this respect has been published recently by Konstantin Raudive, a Latvian psychologist now living in Germany. Raudive has discovered that tapes made by speaking directly into a microphone, by recording from a radio tuned to random "white noise" interference, or by connecting the recorder to a crystal diode set with a very short aerial, all include soft extraneous voices. The voices speak with a strange rhythm in many languages, sometimes so softly that it is

necessary to amplify them by electronic means. Raudive says, 'the sentence construction obeys rules that differ radically from those of ordinary speech and, although the voices seem to speak in the same way as we do, the anatomy of their speech apparatus must be different from our own.' The strangest thing about these recorded voices is that they seem to respond to questions put by Raudive and his collaborators by producing more of their Esperanto-style comments that often look like direct answers.

"In the past six years Raudive has recorded more than seventy thousand conversations of this kind. The speech content of the recordings is exhaustively recounted and analyzed in a book that includes testimonials from very well known and reputable scientists who were either present when the tapes were made or who were able to examine the equipment involved. There can be no doubt about the reality of the sounds; they are on the tapes and can be broken down into phonemes and analyzed by voice-print machinery, but their source is open to question. Raudive believes that man 'carries within himself the ability to contact his friends on earth when he has passed through the transition of death'. In other words, he is certain that the voices are those of the dead, and he confidently identifies some of them as Goethe, Mayakovsky, Hitler, and his own mother. It is difficult to argue with this, because rigidly controlled experiments have been unable to account for the presence of the voices by any normal method.

"On 24 March, 1971 a test was made at the studios of a major recording company in England. Engineers used their own equipment and installed instruments to exclude freak pickups from radio stations and both high and low frequency transmitters. Raudive was not allowed to handle any of the equipment at any time, and a separate, synchronized recording was made of every sound taking place in the studio. During the eighteen-minute recording, both tapes

> were monitored constantly and nothing untoward could be heard, but on playback it was discovered that there were more than two hundred voices on the experimental tape and that some were so clear that they could be heard by everyone present."

I have read Dr. Raudive's book (Breakthrough) where even Vivekananda's voice is registered. Indeed, current American experiments in the field are going beyond the late Raudive's discoveries. We must suspend judgment until all the possible anti-explanations are nullified.

Take, for instance, The Ghost of Flight 401 by John Fuller, an actual aircrash reconstructed with industrious research.

> "In the dead of night in December, 1972, Eastern Airlines jumbo jet Flight 401 plunged into the Florida Everglades killing 101 passengers and crew. Months later, the ghosts of its pilot and flight engineer began to appear on sisterships carrying parts salvaged from the crash...
>
> "After a classic reconstruction of the mysterious crash itself, Fuller interviews scores of airline flight personnel and explores every facet of every 'ghost' report. A rigorous sceptic who has always written with professional thoroughness on all subjects he has undertaken, Fuller ultimately makes personal contact with spirit of the dead flight engineer Don Repo."

My theme is not to propagandize ghost stories but to demand respectful examination of tangible evidence of death, not as a final exit into Nothingness, as superstitious materialists and rationalist ignoramuses facilely dogmatise, but to introduce by this Foreword a book which contains testimony of transmortal communication with mortals. The humility of rationality and the humanism of materialism are, if authentic, never authoritarian enough to claim a monopoly of cosmic holism. Sepulchred science cannot spread its luminous wings unless, fearless of its ayatollahs and mullas, it cares and dares to fly forward into the uninhibited noesis of Light. I have evidence aplenty to prove this thesis but that may be done, if my life, in its last leg, lasts that long, in a separate book. A whole library which tells us how death-life-death continuum can stand the most rigorous tests, experiential and experimental, is now available in many centres. Scientific theory, explanatory of practical observation, can be traced in many countries, including the Soviet Union, the United States and the United Kingdom, to unlock thanatology through psycho-physical processes and tools of new technology. I know there is much chicanery, quackery, charlatanry and sharp practice in this twilight terrain but I do know also of credible, why, even incontestable material to substantiate the case for survival after death and reincarnation. The day is not distant when brave science, giving up obdurate obscurantism and totalitarian materialism, will synthesise Matter and Spirit and evolve the super-physics and super-psychology of Tomorrow by valid thoughtways and techniques which will unravel death, currently regarded as a 'riddle wrapped in a mystery inside an enigma'.

Now let me, with trepidation tempered by certitude, present to you my word of appreciation for the book titled '*The Great Mystery of Life beyond Death*'. Mr. K.H. Kaji, a senior advocate of the Supreme Court and a first-rate tax lawyer of clarity and integrity, who knows my deep interest in the subject of Life, Death and Beyond, has persuaded me to write this Foreword. By sceptical attitude and professional training I resist credulous conclusions and other-worldly abracadabra. But 'death' facts, incontrovertibly probative, command closer investigation and summon unconventional approaches. Kaji and I are possibly on the same wavelength.

The Preface to the book is illuminating and I commend the reader to study it first. Death is always around Life and yet everyone—Gurus included—avoids study of the spiritual chemistry of death and after. Most people are afraid of death, and with escapist bravado, talk lightly of death, the truth being avoidance of what one cannot face. Why not ask, What is Death? What is the law of life after life? The democracy of death is not a frightful torture nor added terror but a meaningful existence on an altered dimension. Death opens unknown doors, ushers us into a different yet evolutionary growth. Radhakrishnan summed up the Indian, yet scientific veiw-point thus:

> "The objective world exists. It is not an illusion. It is real not in being ultimate, but in being a form, an expression of the ultimate. To regard the world as ultimately real is delusion."
>
> (Radhakrishnan, *Eastern Religions & Western Thought*)

Thus, Life and Death move together and each is real, even complementary. Let us know Death better and we then know Life better and plan our terrestrial tenancy better.

The author of this book is not the lawyer Kaji but his father professor Hiralal L. Kaji. The spiritual author of this work is Sir Arthur Conan Doyle. The medium being two others— the son and nephew of the late Kaji. I regard this book as part of that unique literature on Death—not vitiated by wishful thinking nor adulterated by psychic leaning. I will give you the author's own words:

> "No pleasure could be greater than the one I experience in presenting this volume to the public, inasmuch as I was given the unique privilege of expounding *The Great Mystery of Life beyond Death* as unfolded by the spirit of the famous spiritualist, the late Sir Arthur Conan Doyle. I wish to state with all the clearness and sincerity at my command that no single idea expressed in this book is mine and that no single sentence as recorded is mine either. Beyond touching up some loose expressions here and there, the book is presented as spelt out letter by letter on the Ouija Board by the late Sir Arthur through my son Mr. Ashok H. Kaji and my nephew Mr. Subodh B. Kaji. I may as well confess that I have not read hitherto any book on spiritualism, nor have

I read any religious, philosophical or metaphysical books of the Hindus or any other nation for the matter of that. My son is a B.Sc. of the Bombay University and my nephew is an M.Com. of the same University, and neither of them has devoted any thought whatsoever to the problems of the spirit-world and the life beyond death, for as they have repeatedly declared, it is enough if they concentrated on the problems of the life before them in this world of the living instead of dabbling in those of the life in the world of the dead, which might well have an interest for people in the evening of life. I want the public therefore to accept the fact that in this book there is absolutely no contribution of ideas, conscious or sub-conscious, by myself or my son or my nephew, and no contribution to expression, excepting just a little touching up before publication, for I have retainded even some queer and loose expressions.

"The story of this little volume might perhaps be of some interest to the readers. I have always regarded myself as a rather prosaic, matter-of-fact person, not given to indulging in any flights of imagination. I was not conscious of the possession of any spirtitual powers, latent or patent."

My personal conviction about survival is based on varieties of evidence, not faith but proof, not scriptures but records of experiments, not the sorrow of parting but tested material which convinces. But my mission is not proselytisation of the disbeliever. Borrowed conclusions are counterfeit. But a scientific mind should not run away from facts. Edgar D. Mitchell in his introductory article 'Form Outer Space to Inner Space' says what is apt as a concluding thought to my foreword:

'As a student of science, I believe there is nothing in the universe that is unworthy of investigation. If it offers the further incentive of having possible benefit for humanity, I think it is little less than foolish to refuse to examine it. The true scientist is one who is committed to knowing, to scientia, which is the attempt to understand the ultimate nature of reality, without bias, prejudice, or commitment to an ideology or belief system. Otherwise, he is unworthy of the name.'

A more sublime, yet insightful, thought on death cannot be found than in the great verses of Tagore's *Gitanjali*:

> "I was not aware of the moment when I
> first crossed the threshold of this life.
> What was the power that made me
> open out into this vast mystery like a bud
> in the forest at midnight !
> When in the morning I looked upon
> the light I felt in a moment that I was
> no stranger in this world, that the
> inscrutable without the name and form had taken me
> in its arms in the form of my
> own mother.
> Even so, in death the same unknown
> will appear as ever known to me. And
> because I love this life, I know I Shall love
> death as well.
> The child cries out when from the right
> breast the mother takes it away, in the
> very next moment to find in the left one
> its consolation."

Death, I confess, is too deep an issue to dispel the dread and darkness in the minds of men merely by reading one revelatory book from the great Conan Doyle communicated through the late Hiralal L. Kaji. Even so, we must invade ignorance and illumine the subject stage by stage. From that perspective, '*The Great Mystery of Life beyond Death*' is an invaluable start.

"This is not the end. It is not even the beginning of the end. But it is perhaps, the end of the beginning."

(Winston Churchill)

554, Anna Salai,
Teynampet,
Madras-600 018
August 1, 1983

V.R. Krishna Iyer

PREFACE TO THE SECOND REVISED EDITION

It gives us great pleasure to write the Preface to the Second Revised Edition of the book "*The Great Mystery of Life beyond Death*", written by our late father, Prof. H.L. Kaji and published in 1938. After the first edition went out of print, we continued to receive numerous enquiries about the book from many parts of India and abroad, and it was for this reason that a second edition was planned. However, before work on it could commence, our father passed away and the matter was shelved, but enquiries continued to be received.

The subject is one that has always fascinated mankind and interest in it appears to have grown in recent years. We frequently joined our father at the Ouija Board during his lifetime. After his death, the Ouija Board was a source of comfort to us, since we are convinced that our attempts to contact him are successful.

The book remains absorbing although nearly half a century had elapsed since it first appeared. We have therefore not felt it necessary to edit the text in any way and it remains exactly as presented to the public in the first edition.

We are very grateful to Mr. V.R. Krishna Iyer, former Judge, Supreme Court of India, for writing a foreword to this edition. We are sure the Foreword will constitute a significant addition to the book.

"Gangotri"
12, Dhaval Society No. 2
Memnagar Road, Navrangpura
Ahmedabad - 380 009, India

ASHOK H. KAJI
KANISHKA H. KAJI

PREFACE

No pleasure could be greater than the one I experience in presenting this volume to the public, inasmuch as I was given the unique privilege of expounding *The Great Mystery of Life beyond Death* as unfolded by the spirit of the famous spiritualist, the late Sir Arthur Conan Doyle. I wish to state with all the clearness and sincerity at my command that no single idea expressed in this book is mine and that no single sentence as recorded is mine either. Beyond touching up some loose expressions here and there, the book is presented as spelt out letter by letter on the Ouija Board by the late Sir Arthur through my son Mr. Ashok H. Kaji and my nephew Mr. Subodh B. Kaji. I may as well confess that I have not read hitherto any book on spiritualism, nor have I read any religious, philosophical or metaphysical books of the Hindus or any other nation for the matter of that. My son is a B.Sc. of the Bombay University and my nephew is an M.Com. of the same University, and neither of them has devoted any thought whatsoever to the problems of the spirit-world and the life beyond death, for as they have repeatedly declared, it is enough if they concentrated on the problems of the life before them in this world of the living instead of dabbling in those of the life in the world of the dead, which might well have an interest for people in the evening of life. I want the public therefore to accept the fact that in this book there is absolutely no contribution of ideas, conscious or sub-conscious, by myself or my son or my nephew, and no contribution to expression, excepting just a little touching up before publication, for I have retained even some queer and loose expressions.

The Ouija Board is, besides, a fraud-proof apparatus for

spirit-communication. Neither the medium nor the instruments go off into a trance; they are fully conscious and remain just their ordinary selves. There is no darkening of the room, no switching off of lights. The fact that the pointer is touched lightly by one finger of each of the two instruments is a proof of its movement being directed not by them but by the thought impressions produced on the minds of each of them by some outside intelligence from beyond. No two persons can move the pointer in harmony unless each is trying to obey the same impulse of spelling out the same words to express the same impressed thoughts. While therefore the public might remain as sceptical as they choose of the fact of spirit-communication, they should, I beg of them, recognise the fact that there is no fraud or trick, conscious or unconscious, on the preparation of this little volume.

Who dictated or spelt out the letters of the words in the sentences in the book is a question indeed. We are told, the spirit is that of the late Sir Arthur Conan Doyle. If the public want any proof of this, I am sorry, I am not in a position to give it, though I feel convinced that the dictator was Sir Arthur's spirit indeed. It is true that the value of spirit-communication is marred sometimes by the impersonation of the spirit invoked by some frivolously minded or wicked spirit. But, as Sir Arthur pointed out to us, such a possibility cannot be entertained for a moment in this particular case since no spirit would care to impersonate another at more or less regular intervals, over a period extending to about one whole year and that too, not for an amusing chat but for the serious purpose of book dictation, and since the impersonator would not be able to take up the thread just where it was left on the preceding sitting and to make references to phenomena described or explained in preceding chapters. That the style in which the thoughts are expressed is not quite the one, which is so characteristically Sir Arthur's and which is familiar enough to the vast number of the readers of his books on fiction, spiritualism and other subjects, is clear enough. But this, as Sir

Arthur explains, is not in any way strange. He was not writing, but orally dictating without being able to look over the sentences so dictated; sometimes he did ask me to read out what I had written to enable him to pick up the lost thread. The dictation was besides by the conveyance of impressions of thoughts in words to the two young men, being thus restricted by the capacities of Sir Arthur to convey and of Ashok and Subodh to receive the correct impressions and spell them out on the Board. In this process of filtering through the minds of the two instruments, Sir Arthur holds and rightly too, the style gets naturally altered completely. The logic, systematic presentation, analytical ability and experienced exposition, however, clearly reveal a master-writer and trained author, for evidently the two young gentlemen could not possibly, at their age and stage of education, be regarded as capable of producing, in this mysterious joint fashion, a book like this on a subject, on which their minds were a perfect blank. Besides, their obvious reluctance to carry on the work till completion clearly indicates that the thoughts, ideas and explanations emanated from an outside intelligence, we three having nothing to do with these.

The story of this little volume might perhaps be of some interest to the readers. I have always regarded myself as a rather prosaic, matter-of-fact person, not given to indulging in any flights of imagination. I was not conscious of the possession of any spiritual powers latent or patent. I had heard casually of the planchette and of the efforts at spirit-rapping on the three-legged primus stove, furnishing a sabbath occupation to desk-tied and desk-tired clerks. My curiosity however was aroused in 1921 by my sister describing the experiences of a neighbour, who, placing an inverted tiny metallic bowl on a pane of glass and getting each one of a mixed party of five, males and females, to lightly touch it with a finger, saw to his amazement the tiny bowl moving, though very slowly, on the glass surface towards one corner indicating an affirmative or the other corner indicating a negative answer to queries by members of the party. We tried the experiment ourselves with some success; but as we could not get the invoked spirits to spell out any words on the glass on which we pasted slips of paper to represent the letters of the alphabet, we lost interest in about a fortnight and dismissed the matter from our minds.

It was in August 1932 that one evening when the family had gathered after dinner, I told my children of the episode of eleven years back. My offer to try the experiment was welcomed. We began with the fingers of five persons touching the bowl; but as we were getting interested a bit, one of the party had to leave. The remaining four however continued and succeeded in imparting the necessary energy to the bowl to move. This led us to experiment with three and finally with two, Ashok and Subodh. Our progress was rapid and we established communication with our relations, friends, local celebrities and others. We tried to lift the veil of the future too to some extent, though without any great measure of success. We tried to fathom the mysteries of Life beyond Death and gathered some information. Ashok and Subodh tried, and sometimes successfully, to know beforehand questions which were to be asked in their examinations, though on being lectured to on the basic immorality of the desire, they have successfully curbed this instinct so natural to students. A death in the family however upset us and turned our thoughts away from such experiments completely and our spiritual progress was arrested. In May 1935, the insistence of the late Sir Lallubhai Samaldas, a friend, who would not be denied led us to resume our experiments on the Ouija Board, when Sir Arthur Conan Doyle became our spirit guide and friend. Ashok and Subodh rapidly advanced and we had some very remarkable experiences. Sir Chunilal V. Mehta, K.C.S.I. the ex-Finance Member of the Government of Bombay, Sir Lallubhai Samaldas, C.I.E. the well-known co-operator, and industrialist, Sir Prabhashanker Pattani, K.C.S.I., the late septuagenarian Kathiawar statesman, Sir Kikabhai Premchand, a leading financial magnate of Bombay, the Honourable Sheth Shantidas Askuran, Mr. K.L. Panjabi of the Indian Civil Service, and many of our other friends who had sittings on various occasions, enrolled themselves as believers, enthused us and extolled us, and infused us with a sense of the importance of the diffusion of a knowledge of the Great Mystery so as to help clear the confusion that so profusely befogs the vision of people about the life beyond death.

One day, I forget, it was probably sometime in April 1936, Sir Arthur told us that he would be glad to dictate a small book on the Life beyond Death, if we had the patience to take it down. We politely agreed but did not take the proposal quite seriously. A few weeks later, in May, while we were at Mahabaleshwar for the summer, at an evening seance, Sir Arthur asked us: What about the book? I answered with a doubt as to its practicability. He however assured us that the book would be about 150 type-written pages and that he would dictate for two hours on Saturdays and Sundays, so as not to interfere with the studies of my boys. On my agreeing to the idea, he said that he was ready with the outlines of the book. I took paper and pen and jotted down the title page and the synopsis almost exactly as now embodied in the Contents.

The actual dictation of the subject matter was commenced on our return to Bombay in July 1936. Saturdays and Sundays did not prove suitable, however, because of the social and other engagements and two hours at a time proved too much of a strain to Sir Arthur and to the boys. We went on rather irregularly and our average sittings were of about 50 minutes' duration, Sir Arthur dictating about two pages in that time. As the work progressed, the strain on the young gentlemen intensified; but Sir Arthur's persistence and my insistence bore down their resistance and our labours were at last completed at Matheran in May 1937.

I am but a medium and do not therefore desire to expound, comment, analyse or dissect any views or statements in this book. It is possible, several statements may be obscure; several points may have been altogether ignored. But, I know, Sir Arthur wants this volume to be an introduction and not an elaborate treatise expounding the philosophy of the Great Mystery. I therefore venture to publish the volume as it is. But I do wish to assure all genuine serious seekers of truth that any queries for a fuller explanation of some topic, or for information on a point or points ignored in the book will be willingly received and referred to Sir Arthur, who, I have on doubt, will gladly discuss the issues raised. The information thus obtained will be passed on to the inquirer concerned.

If this volume in any way gives to readers a broader and clearer vision of life and its continuity, robs the Dark Unknown of its mystery and Death of its terrors, consoles the bereaved with the prospect of a reunion after death, opens out vistas of interesting speculation about the genesis, purpose of creation, mission of life and the peculiar end—the merger, if this volume helps to prevent the youth from drifting purposeless in life, to protect the adult from the pessimism of failure or the optimism of success and to conjure up before the aged not only pictures of the past but also visions of the future and to afford the scope not only for a contented review of achievements but also for an ambitious programme for further progress, if this volume helps us to attain a clearer notion of spiritualism and spirit-communication by purging the subject of the morbidity that envelopes it, and by urging us on despite our placidity or timidity and helps to thaw the frigidity or neutralise the acidity of our outlook on the Great Problem, our purpose will have been well served and our labour amply rewarded.

I cannot conclude without expressing my sense of deep gratitude to the spirit of the late Sir Arthur Conan Doyle for selecting me as the medium for his mission of service to humanity and for the constant courtesy and fervent friendship which he has ever extended to me. His writings attracted me as a young man and I am very gratified at the reflection that our spirits have much in common and feel attracted to each other so much. I take this opportunity also to tender very humbly and reverently my respectful thanks to Shree Yama Raj for kindly permitting this dictation and publication.

I must also acknowledge with thanks the services rendered by our late friend, Sir Lallubhai Samaldas, without whose insistence, our spiritual activities given up in July 1933 would not have been resumed from May 1935 and without whose active encouragement, we could not have proceeded on with any confidence.

I must also record here my very great appreciation of the faithful and filial service rendered by my son and nephew, without whose close and constant co-operation, despite their preoccupation with their university studies, the production of this volume would have been impossible.

HIRALAL L. KAJI

Cumball Hill
Bombay, India,
Buddha Jayanti,
4th October, 1938

CONTENTS

FOREWORD ...vii
PREFACE TO THE THE SECOND EDITION ...xvii
PREFACE ...xix

INTRODUCTION ...xxxi
Inspiration — Existence of Spirits — Power to Call — Desire to Respond — Different Methods of Response — Automatic writing — Crystal-Gazing—Medium Speaking — Ouija Board: Its Working — Mediums and Instruments — Materialisation — No Telepathy — Spirit and Soul — Idol Worship.

CHAPTER I: DEATH 1
Physical End — The Yama Duta — Forceful Extraction of the Soul — Unnatural Death — Captivity — Ten Days' Abnormal Stay — The Push — Record of Deeds.

CHAPTER II: THE LEAP IN THE DARK 7
Carriage — The Unknown Region — Fast Movement — Bad Treatment — Solitary State — Fatigue — End of the Journey.

CHAPTER III: THE GREAT TRIAL 13
The Patala — The Court — Captives — Yama — Delays — Protracted Trial — Detailed Investigation and Procedure at the Court — Analysis of Human Actions — No Defence — The Ruling — Assignment of Planes — New Births Order — Interval between Successive Births—Unison — Qualities Needed for Progress — Special Treatment: Mediums and Instruments.

CHAPTER IV: THE SEVEN STAGES OR PLANES 31
Location — Presiding Deities.
FIRST PLANE : The Patala — Is it Hell ? — The Court— Elementals — Activity of Spirits — Haunting.

SECOND PLANE : The Bhu Loka — Spirits of Low Order — No Activity — Freedom from Control.
THIRD PLANE : The Tapa Loka — Spirits of Middle Class— Control — Attendance at Trials — Collective Actions — Touch with the World.
FOURTH PLANE : The Chandra Loka — Contented Spirits— Freedom to Move — Touch with Higher Powers — Yama's Visits.
FIFTH PLANE : The Surya Loka — Ambitious Spirits— Administrative Work — Energiser — Presiding Deity.
SIXTH PLANE : The Swarga Loka — Happy Souls — Cold Spirits — Loss of Touch with the World — Loss of Memory.
SEVENTH PLANE : The Deva Loka — God-like Souls — No Touch with Mediums — No Activity — Rest.

CHAPTER V: THE THEORY OF REBIRTH 59
Hindu Belief — Buddhist Doctrine of Karma — Rebirths and Experience — Evolution — Reaping the Fruits of Past Life — Different Types of Births — Number of Births Usually Required for Moksha — Missions of Life — Short Lives and their Missions — Concept of Spirit-identities — Change of Sex.

CHAPTER VI: A DAY IN THE LIFE OF A SPIRIT 75
Environment — No Support Necessary — No Particular Duty— No Physical Senses — No Need for Food or Shelter —Attendance at Trials — Assignment of Special Duties —Attendance on Gods — Petty Investigations — Visit to the World — Peep into the Future — Daily Routine.

CHAPTER VII: THE BONDS WITH THE WORLD 89
Worldly Affections — Change of Sphere after Death — Influence of Planes on Temperament of Spirits — Condition of Feelings before Death — Mediums and Coldness of Spirits — Unfulfilled Desires — Shraddha and the Progress of Spirits — Blood -relations and Friends — Attraction at First Sight.

CHAPTER VIII: THE POWERS AND DISABILITIES OF SPIRITS 99
Mental Powers: General—Elementals and Haunting — Evil Consequences of Help from Elementals — Ordinary Spirits — Higher Spirits : Inspiration — Advice — Guesses about Future

—Access to Divine Souls — Medium's Influence — Materialisation — Details of Next Birth — Attendance on Mediums--Vision— Production of Sound — Memory — Knowledge of Past Birth— Transmission of News — Boons — Spirits among Themselves —Impersonation and Misleading.

CHAPTER IX: THE FINAL GOAL 115

Aim of Life in Worldly Sense — Idea of Karma — Reincarnation — Ambition — Moksha — Merger, the Peculiar End — Longevity of Life — God — Form — Residence — Powers — Darshan — Relation to other Gods — The Creator Vs. Yama — Final Influence over the World —Purpose of Creation.

INDEX 131

INTRODUCTION

Inspiration — Existence of Spirits — Power to Call — Desire to Respond — Different Methods of Response : Automatic Writing — Crystal-Gazing—Medium-Speaking — Ouija Board: Its Working — Mediums and Instruments — Materialisation — No Telepathy — Spirit and Soul — Idol Worship.

Inspiration: Many spirits like myself have in the past made attempts to unfold the mysteries which exist after the physical end of life, but without success, as the mediums through whom they sought to communicate these mysteries to the world of the living usually got tired and gave up their work. I had the same experience myself some time back, but I hope this second attempt of mine becomes successful. In this case, I feel I have found a suitable medium and it is this circumstance that inspires and impels me to take up this difficult task.

Existence of Spirits: One of the most controversial questions is the existence of life beyond death. A few decades back, the civilised world laughed at the idea of spirit and communication with the dead was regarded as only foolish. Very recently however a great change is in evidence. Spiritualism has attracted many amateurs as mediums and these have tried to give to the world some idea of spirits. Seances have revealed such facts that even the most sceptical are forced to admit the existence of such beings and supernatural powers.

Power to Call: One is naturally inclined to ask why if such beings can and do exist, it should not be feasible for all persons to talk with them. The reply to such a query is that spirits are not human beings and some special powers are therefore required in the person who seeks to enter into communication with them. To define such powers is not free from difficulties, as three out of every five mediums are known to practise fraud. However, it can safely be asserted that such powers are latent in most men and can best be developed by practice.

Desire to Respond: In the world of the living, there is a strong belief that the dead are not ready and willing to mix with the living; but it may be pointed out that such a notion is quite incorrect and that the holders of such a view are grossly mistaken. As a matter of fact spirits are rather anxious to enter into communication with human beings. It is only when a considerable time has elapsed, after their passing away from this life, that their desire to meet and talk with the living gets weakened. Further, many persons who have had the chance of seeing or of talking with spirits do not hold conversation with them properly. Here it is the fault of the living rather than of the dead. The unsatisfactory nature of the conversation with spirits at the first sitting need not discourage the medium or his client; for when sittings are numerous, the results are much better.

Different Methods of Response—Automatic Writing: Mediums have continually tried to devise various methods to be in effective touch with the spirit-world: but none so far has reached perfection. To review a few of these methods, there is the method known as 'Automatic Writing'. The words are self-explanatory. In this case, the medium is supposed to invoke the desired spirit through his spirit control. Such a spirit control is usually his friend and assists him in establishing contact with desired spirits. When the spirit is invoked, the medium begins to receive impressions and the manifestation of these impressed thoughts makes the shape of letters of the alphabet forming words and sentences. But to the audience it appears as if the medium is writing down his own thoughts in the ordinary way, instead of the thoughts impressed upon him by the spirit invoked. It may be made clear at this juncture that some mediums of this class are genuine; but there are some who practise fraud, so that it is difficult to separate the genuine from the fraudulent, the wheat from the chaff.

Crystal-Gazing: Another method usually spoken of in connection with spirit-communication is the one known as 'Crystal-Gazing'. This method is of Indian origin. In the time of the Moguls, it found favour with at least the Muslim population. The mechanism is very simple. A glass ball, say of 6 inches diameter is needed. The person who possesses the Power of gazing can see in the crystal the events which are likely to occur within a reasonable time. Crystal-gazing is merely an attempt to foretell the future, this being accomplished by the help of such spirits who can guess the future with approximate correctness. But the idea of holding conversations of other nature with spirits is not developed in this method. Whatever may be the state of development of crystal-gazing in Mogul times, it must be acknowledged that it is at present in a deplorable state and should be abandoned for all practical purposes of spirit-communication.

Medium-Speaking: Moreover, 'Automatic Writing and Crystal-Gazing' are in a way very slow for rapid communication between the spirit-world and the world of the living. To remedy this shortcoming, therefore, mediums after receiving the impressions from the spirit invoked often give them publicity through their own speech. Thus, so far as this method of 'Medium-Speaking' is concerned, there is no tardiness or delay, for the spirit invoked is able to express his ideas easily and rapidly through the impressions he implants on the medium. Like the previous methods, this method also is not above fraud. The speed with which the conversation takes place often makes it impossible for the spirit concerned to give out his impressions to the medium, inasmuch as spirits require some time to mould their views in proper sentences. At any rate, remarkable speed is achieved and for all practical purposes, therefore, this method of medium speaking must be regarded as a fairly good method.

Ouija Board—Its Working: Coming now to the most current system of spirit-communication, we have an arrangement called the Ouija Board. In a crude state, it consists of a board with the letters of the alphabet arranged on its borders. In the case of a well-prepared board, we usually have a circular board with a glass covering. The letters look very decent if they are in black and white. To operate the Board, we use a wooden piece of say one inch diameter. The medium receives the impressions from the spirit invoked and communicates these impressions by moving the wooden piece to the various letters of the alphabet forming words and sentences. The glass covering reduces friction to a minimum and enables great speed to be achieved and makes rapid communication possible. In most cases, the medium is able to operate the Board himself, and the speed with which the Board can function largely depends on the powers of the medium to receive and transmit the messages received from the spirits. Usually the Ouija Board makes it possible to have a good talk with the desired spirit. Sometimes however the medium himself is not able to operate the Board and requires the help of one or more persons as instruments for the purpose. The possibility of fraud is therefore present in this system if the medium functions both as the medium and as the instrument. But if these two are separate people, the dangers of fraud or any such underhand means are largely obviated.

Medium and Instruments: Many persons who can invoke spirits think that they possess mediumistic powers; but all such persons are not mediums in themselves. Some are born mediums and some achieve mediumship through laborious practice. A person who is a strong-willed man and who can attract spirits is a genuine medium. There is some natural force in them that makes the spirits obey their call. In case of weak mediums, we find that all their sittings are not successful, the underlying cause being that their power is not strong enough. A person who is ordinarily likely to give weight to others' views and who is fairly intelligent makes a good instrument, what being chiefly required of him being a good receptive brain. Weaker mediums are instruments themselves as well; but the stronger the medium, the weaker is the power of functioning as his own instrument and very strong mediums are helpless without their instruments. To make the idea clearer, one might conceivably say that the spirits are the electric light bulbs, the medium is the main electric power, which can light bulbs and the instruments are the switch, without turning which on, no contact can be established between the light-bulbs and the electric energy. The presence of one instrument or two coupled with a medium makes the system fraud-proof. The fact that three persons are thus associated in the operation of the Ouija Board should allay suspicions in the minds of even the most sceptical people, inasmuch as three persons cannot form a conspiracy among themselves, insofar as no two people can agree in marshalling out a certain sentence.

Materialisation: In the present state of affairs, it is very difficult to say whether there are any mediums who can materialise spirits. But it is agreed, at the same time, on all hands, that spirits do materialise. Human beigns have a very hazy notion of 'materialisation'. So far, it was held that spirits have no shape; and this holds good even today. But when materialisation does take place, the vapour in the atmosphere gets condensed and gives rise to a form resembling a human being. We must realise thus that materialisation is possible only if there are powerful spirits and if a suitable atmosphere is in existence. Seances have revealed that most spirits are not in a position to get the necessary vapour around them. To add to this, it is recognised that a special power is necessary for materialisation and that power is very rare. The effects of materialisation are not good insofar as it tends to draw away a spirit from his own sphere; and further it is not good for the medium either, because it results in a consumption of his mental energies. The Indian idea that it is not desirable to wean away spirits back to the material world applies correctly in this case, and a time will come when that idea will gain acceptance even amongst western mediums as they are gradually feeling that this mode of communication does not find favour with spirits.

No Telepathy: Even the most intelligent observer has tried to correlate spiritualism with some branch of psychology. In this science, which relates to the unconscious mind and its effects, we find that large powers are attributed to human minds. One of the most important of these powers is that of thought-reading and thought-transfer. We know however that this power is not found in normal cases, and to say that spiritualism is but developed telepathy is far from truth. The simpler course is to believe in the existence of spirits and to regard the Board as a receiving set and to consider the instruments as the transmitting apparatus, the medium being an exchange operator. This in a nutshell explains this supernatural phenomenon. The Ouija Board has no connection whatsoever with telepathy but it is a pure and simple telephone service.

Spirit and Soul: Many would like to think of spirits as ghosts which are described in fiction; but I, as a spirit, can assure you that a ghost is an 'elemental' and therefore not a spirit. Spirits have no body, nor any shape; they are a mere energy as distinguished from mere conception. It is certainly not matter as none of the properties of matter are present in spirits. The Spirit however must not be confounded with the 'soul'. A fine line of difference exists between spirits and souls. Both are not human. That which takes birth is the soul; but the part which remains in the upper world is the spirit. Thus, soul and spirit mean one and the same thing in popular parlance, but if viewed from a spiritual angle of vision, the identity of soul in the spirit-world is the spirit.

Idol Worship: In the East especially, we meet with 'idol worship'. The idea underlying is not easily grasped by western people. Those who are gifted with powers of concentration need who are gifted with powers of concentration need not have an idol before them; but those who form the masses require something before them to enable them to concentrate for a short while at least on things other than those of the world. Most Hindus believe that idol worship is the golden path for attaining salvation; but the notion is hardly correct. It must be admitted however that it tends to make a man spiritually minded and in my opinion, that is the function of idol worship, insofar as it puts the worshipper in direct touch with superior beings, and insofar as it is a good method of spirit-communion if not of spirit communication.

CHAPTER I

DEATH

Physical End—The Yama Duta—Forceful Extraction of the Soul—Unnatural Deaths—Captivity — Ten days' Abnormal Stay — The Push — Record of Deeds.

Physical End

Every man is called a mortal, because no person is free from the monster of Death. The incident of Death is always novel, even though it occurs in all the births which the soul has to undergo. No living being can imagine the real significance of Death. It is really a singular event in one's life. The incident does not occur at any particular age, but its time varies widely. What rules govern this variation of the age at Death will be dealt with subsequently. But this much can be said that Death overpowers a person in his weak state, for when the health is bad, it is very easy to bring about the physical end of life. One might perhaps wonder why it is that men are horrified at the idea of Death. Probably it is due to the realisation that Death means the end of one's life and that what is to come is unknown. Thus, the closing period of a person's life is far from peaceful, for he is found perpetually worrying about the future of his own self. This however in no way stops Death from having its sway.

The Yama Duta

When the time for leaving the world comes, the Yama's Court orders a certain spirit to take charge of the soul concerned. Those spirits who are hard-hearted and who have retained some powers resembling physical force are asked to take up this sort of work. So far as I know, no spirit likes the job, and the drafting of spirits to this service becomes in consequence something in the nature of conscription. Such conscripted spirits have got to perform this unpleasant duty assigned to them by the Yama Raj, the God of Death. This messenger is popularly known as the "Yama Duta". He actually comes to the world while other spirits do not do so usually.

Forceful Extraction of the Soul

It is indeed a very difficult task for the Duta to take away the soul of a human being. His powers are also not strong enough to combat with the human force; but at this time 'Yama Raj' himself imparts the necessary force and this liberates the soul from the body. This force of the God of Death may well be termed the 'Death Ray'. Scientists have striven for years to find out the nature of this force but so far they have not got any clue. It is a supernatural force which shall remain beyond the scope of science. The effect of this ray is severe indeed, insofar as it tends to break up the whole body into pieces. Every limb feels the acute agony of piercing pain. The body has to remain under its influence till it gives way. The struggle is very hard and lasts for a pretty long time, but it invariably leads to the success of Death through the over-dominating influence of Yama's powers. In most cases, we find that the soul is very reluctant to leave the body and the soul has to be extracted forcibly by the Death Messenger. The soul is a sort of energy and it is endowed with a considerable amount of force. The tussle is therefore protracted. If somehow or other the Death Ray is not liberated the Duta is helpless but instances of such mismanagement are few and far between. The soul is very often given a fair chance to close its bodily existence peacefully; but almost invariably the opportunity is not availed of and use of force is inevitable.

It is commonly believed among the Hindus that the dying person sees or feels the presence of the Yama Duta and reveals his consciousness of the presence by agonised shrieks or tortuous bewilderment. The dogs in the vicinity set up a series of mournful howls due, it is held, to their uncanny sixth sense which makes them conscious of the presence of the Messenger of Death. It has been further commonly held that in the case of a saintly or good soul, the Duta is unable to seize the soul and Yama Raj himself has to come down to achieve the purpose. The legend of Satyavan and Savitri speaks of the strong will and soul force of the pure and devoted wife which rendered the Duta helpless and compelled the presence of Yama Raj himself. Savitri is said to have followed Yama Raj who was dragging away the soul of her husband Satyavan in a net for miles, whether physically or otherwise we are not told and won back her lord from Yama Raj's clutches by her soft pleadings and devoted remonstrance. All that is however not correct. Apparently there is a glimmer of truth when the forceful extraction of the soul, its captivity and the last journey of the soul are alluded to. But it never is necessary for the God of Death himself to come down for the extraction of the soul. His Death Ray is quite sufficient for the purpose.*

Unnatural Death

It has been remarked above that before Death overtakes a person, it is essential that weakness of some sort or the other must overpower him. This weakness may take various forms. It might be physical weakness or it might be mental; it might affect the senses or it might affect the sensibilities, the emotions. Thus, when a person ends his physical existence voluntarily by suicide, there is the weakness of the mind or of the emotions, which makes him overwrought or high-strung and throws him out of balance. An accident is the result of some conscious or subconscious absent-mindedness, which is thus a form of weakness inviting the presence of the Yama Duta followed by the liberation of the Death Ray by Yama Raj at the proper moment. Thus in all cases of deaths, whether a person is good or sinful, whether he dies a lingering or a sudden

* As a result of a discussion with Sir Arthur, I wrote out this paragraph, read it over to him and with his approval added it here.

or voluntary death, the God of Death sends his Messenger and the soul is forcibly extracted from its bodily tenement.

Captivity

After the long drawn struggle, life in the body becomes extinct and the soul comes out exhausted and haggard. It is very easy for the Duta now to capture the soul which is weak. This captivity is a unique one in so far as there is no physical captivity. The effect of the Death Ray is still very strong and there is no need to capture the soul by any device. When thus captured, the soul is not free to do all things which he might desire. He has to obey all the orders of the Duta. There is however only one freedom of action during the captivity of the soul and that is that he can move about among his relatives. In normal circumstances, he should not, during this period, respond to calls of mediums. If any such attempt is made, however, he will not be allowed the liberty of moving about among his family. This sort of captivity lasts for ten days. It is a period of great hardship as the attitude of the Yama Duta is very stern and every breach of rules is directly reported forthwith to the Court authorities.

Ten Days' Abnormal Stay

The struggle of Death is over and bodily existence is a thing of the past. The soul is in an extremely perturbed state. The links with the world are yet fresh before him and he is all the while lamenting over his failure to resist Death. To add poignancy to his grief, he witnesses his own burial or cremation ceremony and such other allied functions. If the soul concerned has relatives, their lamentations and mourning make him completely restless, for he is at once cut off from them and from the world of the living. The shock is so severe that it is very painful for him to stay any longer. But he is compelled to do so and that too for a good cause. During these days, he has got to learn to overcome feelings and sentiments. He is among the people he loved most and yet he is denied the power to talk with them. He is in a place where eatables are in plenty and yet he no access to them. In this way, he has to learn many things and to acquire varied experiences. It is the duty of the Duta to take the soul to various places, which would tempt him and in this manner study his character. Acid tests of all types are applied during this period. At the end of this period, the duty of the Duta is over and the soul is handed over to another spirit who has to take him to the spirit-world. It is interesting to note that only ten days are reserved for a stay in this world after Death. The first three days are used up in attending the funeral ceremonies; the next four days are necessary for testing the soul by the Duta in various ways, while the remaining three days are granted to the soul to see his relatives and to settle down. Further some souls need to be instructed by the Duta before they leave for the next world. They are coached up about their journey to the next world. Before I touch upon the next point, it should be made clear that in the Hindu religion we find that there exists a belief that the soul is kept lingering on in the world, but the theory does not give the above-stated reasons. it is sad to note that other religions have no ideas about such existence after death and much less about Rebirth.

The Push

The old Yama Duta leaves the soul at this stage as his responsibility is over. He hands over the soul to another spirit, who is in charge of the transport department of Yama Raj. He is a spirit who has force enough to lead the soul through the most complex journey which the soul has to undertake. He has got abnormal speed. He is said to have a speed of 100 miles per hour. All the while, he drags the soul in an extremely rough manner. He knows no respect, on merit, and shows no kindness. He is taking the soul as if he was carrying bundles of goods instead of one of God's creations. Now we shall see how he gives momentum to the fagged-out inert soul. When he deems it expedient, he summons the winds to his aid. A very strong gale puts the soul in a state which is essential for speedy transport. This moment is the final one, so far as the present birth is concerned.

Record of Deeds

Before we conclude this chapter I think a description of the recording of the deeds of the soul concerned should be given. No sooner does the soul come out from the body than he is asked to give out all he knows about himself. Of course, there is no speech but the thoughts expressed are received by the Duta. It is then the duty of the Messenger of Yama to transmit the relevant features of the soul's doings, to the principal Court. There the spirits in charge record the information received on the layers of air. These records are useful at the Trial. In the next chapter, we shall speak of the unique journey which lasts for nearly ten days.

CHAPTER II

THE LEAP IN THE DARK

Carriage — The Unknown Region — Fast Movement — Bad Treatment — Solitary State — Fatigue — End of the Journey.

Carriage

The soul being blown up by a gust of wind is in a proper condition to commence his travel to the 'Satya Darbar' or the 'final tribunal'. The spirit-in-charge now assumes full possession of the soul and towards that purpose he proceeds to rob him of his valuable power of vision. The poor soul is as it were thus blindfolded and thrown upon the tender mercies of the spirit from whom he is obliged to seek help. The deprivation of the power of sight by the spirit appears rather strange for one does not understand its proper significance. Spirits in general do not and this spirits of the Transport Department in particular does not possess any power to control a soul and it is probably this that makes recourse to this indirect method of obtaining full control over him necessary on the part of the spirit. With the soul thus rendered helpless, the spirit begins to perform his most important duty and moves further and further from the world. His movement is of two kinds. In the beginning, it is that of climbing higher and higher and afterwards it usually takes a westerly direction.

The Unknown Region

While climbing, we leave the world behind and move in an upward direction. The region which the soul has to traverse is our atmosphere: but it is the worst possible region as we shall see subsequently. The first few miles are tolerable insofar as the stormy elements are of a mild nature. When this distance is covered, a halt is ordered by the Yama's Court. The spirit is allowed to restore the sight to the soul, the idea underlying being to test the soul. But as soon as the sight is thus restored, the soul makes an attempt to go back to his old world and it is rare to find a soul who can curb such a very natural desire. The consequences of such attempts are however very serious in view of the fact that the soul is at once ordered to tour round the world. The spirit thereupon takes him to the old world again and the tour commences. The time allotted for the whole journey is very limited and to incorporate this extra tour of about 25,000 miles in the programme means a great deal of extra trouble and hardship. It is, therefore, very advisable to control one's own desire to return back to the world and thereby avoid the extra discomfort and untold miseries and troubles attendant upon a whirl round in a world tour. The journey is now resumed and the region becomes positively bad and terrifying. Darkness benumbs the soul bereft as he is of his power of sight; the atmosphere after a certain height becomes very uncomfortable and, despite what science might hold, storms of all types are perpetual; thunder and lightning make bad matters further worse for the poor dragged soul to withstand and the fears of the unknown add to the horrors of the journey which no power of the pen can effectively and vividly portray.

Fast Movement

The distance to be accomplished is long, very long and the time allotted is usually ten days, much too short for the distance. A high degree of speed therefore becomes absolutely essential and the extra world tour imposes a greater obligation to achieve still higher speeds. The spirit moves fast and yet faster and the poor soul is towed, is dragged along, at the same speed amidst the gloom and impenetrable darkness, which the absence of vision entails and which appears most bewildering, terrifying and frightful. There is no groping about in the dark; there is rather a wild and mighty and furious rush. To the soul, this is a very severe trial indeed. With the forced severance from his earthly tenement, from the relatives, friends and companions he was so closely associated in life with, with the captivity and the ten days' abnormal stay after Death, this exceedingly fast movement is intensely nerve-racking.

Bad Treatment

The spirit-in-charge is perpetually dissatisfied with the soul as he is not able or rather does not attempt to follow him; and this results in the manifestation of a very severe and hostile attitude on the part of the spirit. Every time the soul grumbles about the speed, the spirit gets extremely angry and instead of slackening the speed ever so little, accelerates it. He is not amenable to reason or argument but acts in a truly despotic fashion. Many times during the journey, the soul requests him to restore his power of sight; but he does not even soothe the poor soul, who, to add to his difficulties, does not know when the journey would end or the moment when his sight would be restored. Suspense in the mind of the soul tends to retard his speed which in its turn invites rebukes and castigation from the spirit-in-charge. Even towards the end of the journey, the spirit does not become in any way friendly but continues to be as taciturn and harsh as ever. Sometimes when it becomes absolutely essential to stop, he does so very reluctantly and that too for a very short period. This sort of attitude appears to me to be very strange. The soul should not be treated in such an outrageous fashion in so far as he has committed no fault. Another thing that strikes me is that the duration of the travel can be easily increased in view of the fact that the distance to be covered is enormous. Furthermore the tour round the world, a feature of a very large percentage of such journeys of souls after death is redundant as the soul without the power of vision cannot gain anything from such a tour. In my discussion with Yama Raj, however, I have gathered that the tour is not for pleasure or education but is merely intended as a punishment, to the unchastened soul, whose longings for the world he has left have not yet lost their strength and intensity, for not curbing his desire to go back. In some cases, when the soul absolutely refuses to obey the orders of the spirit or refuses to move, the only course left open for the spirit is to inform the Court about the recalcitrancy of the soul. The Court will then liberate a speed-ray, which 'would drag the soul to his final destination'.

Solitary State

It happens in many cases that the soul takes a defiant attitude and harasses the spirit-in-charge in many ways. All such attempts on the part of the soul however lead to disastrous consequences; and yet we find that as many as forty per cent of the souls try thier level best to tease, vex and obstruct the spirit-in-charge. At first the spirit tries to ignore such acts, but when they become too frequent, he takes notice of them and warns the soul. In some cases this has no effect and the spirit ultimately gets tired and sick of such a soul; but being afraid of reporting such matters too often to the Court, he employs another device and that is of disappearing from the ken of the soul and thereby leaving him to look after himself in the impenetrable darkness. The soul who is bereft of sight and who for the time being is thus left in very complex and difficult circumstances realises now his own faults; but this repentance on his part does not evoke any sympathy from the spirit-in-charge, who continues to leave him in solitude. The soul has to brood over his mistakes, for even three days in some cases, after which the spirit returns refreshed to resume the journey. This solitary state is perhaps the most difficult time for the soul, as he is left bewildered in most dangerous surroundings. It must be made clear that those souls who behave well and are obedient are of course not left in the lurch by the spirit. It is therefore very advisable for the soul not to flout the authority of or cause annoyance to the spirit, for, otherwise, apart from the absence of any good will on the part of the spirit, he will encounter positive harshness and will have to undergo the utterly demoralising experience of the solitary state.

Fatigue

After the solitary soul gets his guide again, he begins to proceed further on his weary way. At first, the soul is also refreshed as he had a compulsory stoppage for two or three days. His guide is however much more refreshed as he had a nice rest when the soul was left alone. The excessive fatigue which has been accumulating during the journey makes it nearly impossible for the soul to follow the spirit who is now actually running faster to make up for the three days which were wasted in bringing the soul to his senses. The soul, who is not in a position to even drag along, cannot possibly keep pace with the spirit. But anyhow the soul has to follow the spirit, because if he does not do so he would not be able to reach in time. He has got to be present in the Court before the period of ten days is over. The fatigue is so pressing that the soul is often forced to request the spirit-in-charge to stop for a while but the request in most cases receives scant attention and passes off unheeded by the spirit.

The deprivation of the power of sight, the long-drawn journey, the terrors of an unknown region, fast locomotion, unsympathetic and harsh treatment from his guide, the solitary state which more often than not the soul has to face and the unimaginable fatigue and exhaustion are features of this Leap into and Rush throught the Dark which make the final journey of the soul the most unique and inconceivable even under the incubus of a frightful nightmare.

All souls have to traverse the same region and follow the same identical track with so many persons dying at about the same time, so many souls are travelling towards the same destination accompanied by their respective guides, and the traffic along the route is heavy indeed. But the souls being without the power of sight do not see any other souls or their guides overtaking them or being overtaken by them nor are they conscious about them. Each soul is absorbed in and is conscious only of his own problem and his own self heedless of what might be happening to others similarly stituated.

End of the Journey

About nine days are used up in reaching the Yama's Court. But the spirit-in-charge does not go to the Court with the soul. When it is about five miles or so, he leaves him alone and hurries up to the Court and informs the spirits who happen to be there that a particular soul has come near them. If the soul was a person who had achieved fame, many spirits go to receive him. If he was not a known man, hardly a few would care to receive him except his near relatives. So far, the soul was not in a position to meet any one; but now as he is relieved of the control of the spirit, he is able to mix with those who come near him. His eyesight is as it were restored, because he is able to see not physically but as spirits do. The soul becomes buoyant and gay, as he happens in most cases to be among his relatives and friends.

Now at last the fast movement is at an end and the lessening of fatigue is a great relief to the dragged soul. His friends take him very quietly and slowly to the Court. But the soul begins to get uneasy about his impending trial. The soul is not yet entitled to enter the Yama's Court. He has to procure a permit to enter this divine tribunal where his case is to be decided. The spirit-in-charge usually during this period procures the permit and takes the soul in the Court where he is to await his trial. Control over the soul is now very nominal and he is at liberty to act according to his sweet will, the only reservation being that he has to attend the Court during office-hours.

CHAPTER III

THE GREAT TRIAL

The Patala — The Court — Captives — Yama — Delays — Protracted Trial — Detailed Investigation and Procedure at the Court — Analysis of Human Actions — No Defence — The Ruling — Assignment of Planes —New Birth Order — Interval between Successive Births — Unison — Qualities Needed for Progress — Special Treatment: Mediums and Instruments.

The Patala

The place where Yama holds his Court is known in Hindu mythology as Patala. The word ordinarily signifies the underworld, or even the antipodes. The idea of an underworld is common among the Christians too and the underworld of Satan compares to some extent with the popular idea of Yama's region. But as a matter of fact, the conceptions of Yama and Satan are radically different.

This important region is situated about a few hundred miles from the world of human beings and is certainly composed of the atmosphere; but the density of the air pervading there as compared with the air in other parts of the spirit world reminds one of the air conditions in mines. The air is very heavy and makes it rather uncomfortable for the spirits and souls, though they do not inhale any air whatsoever. The area of this first plane is very large, nearly half of our world. Even though such a large space is reserved for new spirits as well as for old ones, it is always heavily crowded with all sorts of spirits and souls. The Patala is roughly divided into two parts one for Court purposes and the other for spirits who are classed as elementals and there is a great insurmountable barrier between these two parts of the region.

The soul who was about five miles away is gradually brought into this region and is admitted to the Court section of this place. He is fairly comfortable in the new world, as he is among such souls and spirits as were familiar to him, prior to this departure from his old world. The trial does not begin at once, and this is a relief to him insofar as he is not prepared to face it, after such a lengthy and tiring journey. Gradually he fits into the new and peculiar order of things at the Court. It is assumed here the word Court includes the area adjoining the Court proper which is utilized for accommodating souls awaiting trials and also those who feel like witnessing the daily proceedings.

The Court

So far we have spoken of the region as such. We shall now however speak of the Court with Yama at its head. As we have seen before, the Court is in the plane called the Patala and extends to about half of the total area of the plane. Sixty per cent of this area however is reserved for souls awaiting their own trial; while the other forty per cent is the part set apart for the actual Court. The daily proceedings are conducted here and the Chief Justice, or to express it in the terms current here, the Yama Raj, is at the head. In the centre, the 'Yama' takes his seat. It would appear to some that there would be some concrete sitting accommodation, but such an illusion should not be maintained, as there are no such facilities nor are they necessary in view of the fact that there is no longer any physical existence there.

Just near the God of Justice, are found spirits who are in charge of the records of all souls. The record keepers are classified into two major groups, one doing the actual work of recording, after receiving the requisite information from the spirits-in-charge who send on such information shortly after a person dies. The other section of the record keepers does the work of transcribing the records when evidence is sought from them by the prosecutor at the time of the trial.

Just behind these record keepers, there are about a hundred spirits who specialise in procuring any further information in case the record proves inadequate. These spirits are of a very high order and they possess the very rare quality of deduction from the scanty material which may be available to them.

Soon after we leave this group of spirits, we find ourselves among so-called specialists who out of philanthropy wish to plead for those souls who in their opinion deserve such help. But all spirits cannot act as 'counsel' unless they are permitted by the Yama-in-Council. The merits necessary for holding such an honorary post are never explained; but if I may be allowed to surmise, a clear-cut idea of important problems affecting souls would qualify one to be elected as one of such celebrated spirits. Their work is not selfless in the sense that they, usually, after some time request Yama to promote them to better planes.

Then on the left side of Yama we see the prosecutor, with a few assistants to help him in his laborious task. Near these spirits, we have a score of 'attendants' who bring the souls according to the numbers allotted to them. The attendants are not in any way the servants of Yama's Court. They are requested to work only for a comparatively short time after which period a new batch is substituted in their place. In this way, this part of the Court work is carried on by the temporary services of spirits.

So far we have dealt with some of the most important officials who are usually found in the Court. It will have been seen that the Court of the spirits resembles in many respects the courts in the human world. Of course, there are some points of difference which however will be dealt with subsequently. Over and above the space for these officials, there is an area reserved for other spirits who desire to see the proceedings of the Court. The usual attendance is very large as most spirits utilise their leisure time in the Court, though there are some spirits who never like to attend the Court with the result that they have a very defective knowledge of the spirit-world.

Captives

So far we have only looked at the officials of the Court; but there are the souls who have come from the world very recently. These are strictly under the supervision of spirits-in-charge of these captives. They are awaiting their trial and are very anxious to have the trial commence at once. All the while, they are in a very perturbed state of mind, for they feel just like persons in a law court in the presence of the Chief Justice. Such a state of mind is the natural outcome of the circumstances which prevail there. It is very kind on the part of the Court authorities to allow all such souls to mix with one another. This helps to reduce the agony and discomfort which a soul is likely to experience. Yama however does not desire the new comers to be in a position to know all the laws which are applied in giving the final decision and does not therefore allow these souls to mix with spirits after the first twenty-four hours are complete. A shrewd soul can get almost complete information about the rules in force there during this period; but most souls while away their time in talking on other subjects, little knowing that after a day they will not be allowed to talk with the spirits. In this case, they are captives as this restriction is meant to exclude them from the spirit world. In other respects, however, they are completely free, as they are even allowed to talk through their medium if they have any.

The number of such souls is very large as all the souls who arrive there on a particular day are not dealt with on the same day. The arrears gradually accumulate and this makes it necessary for the Court to work overtime.

Yama

The whole Court centres around the pivot called the God of Death or 'Dharma Raj'. In the popular mind, he is the terrifying Yama. He is said to have held this post of extreme responsibility from the very beginning or the evolution of mankind. He is an Eternal Being, free from the coveted 'moksha' or Merger. He ranks equally with the conception of God, the Creator. Sometimes he interferes in the work of creation too, which is the sole province of God. Similarly God also if he thinks it expedient interferes in the decisions given by Yama. However, it must be stated that both of them are free to hold their own if it becomes a matter of principle. But naturally they adopt the principle of 'give and take'. Yama has three rays: the one which we have already described in the 'death ray' a most important weapon in his hands. The other ray is the 'speed ray' which has the power or strength of attracting and dragging any object to him. The third and the final ray is the 'life ray', which is used when the soul has to take birth. In these three rays, one can see the extent and importance of the powers vested in Yama. The Life Ray has the power to give life to a dead person. But Yama is very reluctant to use his third ray and this often brings him in conflict with the Creator, who needs that ray for his work of creation.

In Indian mythology, Yama is depicted as the God without a heart. His sternness however is not real but is the quality attributed to him by the imagination of men. He is really a kind-hearted god with a keen sense of justice which would not be tempered by any other consideration except the merits of the case. It is this ideal sense of impartiality on the part of Yama which tends to give an impression of sternness in him. It is however true that he never grants life to a soul who is to leave the world at a certain date. Only in case when justice demands a revision of the term of years granted he would change his decision on that matter. Yama is the most highly honoured god in this spirit-world. Yet it is rather strange that in the land of idolworshippers, Yama has no place. He is also the most hard working and active god and I think he really ought to be worshipped by all who believe in idols.

His circle of influence is very great in the Patala, but this region should not be confounded with Hell. The region over which the Yama rules is the Court in a wider sense. With the so-called Hell, he has nothing to do. Yama is the symbol of

Energy and Power, as he never seems to get tired; but he is all the while quite fresh. His hours of work in the Court are from morning eight to evening nine, with a few hours of rest during the day-time. Even after that, he is expected to discuss certain points with his chosen few. The work is completed in an hour or so. In the matter of judgment, he does not believe in the English theory of expediting the investigation of cases; but he thinks twice before he gives out his mind, and instructs his spirits to follow his advice. From all points of view, he is regarded as the most suitable divinity to handle this part of the administration in the spirit world. To some minds it may not appear that Yama is impartial; but so far as I am able to judge, he tries to be impartial though he may bestow some favour in cases where there is sufficient justification for being so kind. Such actions are very often misconstrued and give rise to the opinion that in some cases proper justice is not administered.

Delays

In the morning the Court opens, that is, it begins to function; there are, of course, no doors to be thrown open. There are some spirits, whose duty it is to allot numbers to the new comers. The basis on which these numbers are assigned is quite logical. The number of the plane in which the spirits of the souls reside is found out and out of souls of the same plane, the principle of first come, first served is adopted, Thus, the spirits of higher planes are taken up first for their trial. It may be indicated here that the number of new comers exceeds the number of cases disposed of during a particular day. This is one of the most important causes of delay which is proverbially long. I had a talk with Yama himself and I suggested that there should be more judges like Yama himself; but he promptly said that equality of justice was to be maintained at any cost. I added that a little sacrifice could be permitted for the sake of the convenience of many souls who were daily eagerly awaiting their trial. Yama refused however to discuss the matter any further and I had to keep quiet. It appears that the question which confronts him is not one of the balance of justice but of the balance of power between such Yamas, though there may be also the difficulty of Justice being systematic and uniform. To get a clear idea of the whole procedure, we might take a concrete case.

In the case of a soul, who comes to the spirit world, the spirit, who allots numbers, finds out the plane in which his spirit rests. Supposing he is in the fourth plane, his rank will be low, as spirits of higher planes will get precedence. Furthermore, among the spirits of the same plane, all rush up to the spirit who allots numbers and quiet souls who cannot get a number which is so necessary to expedite the trial have to wait fairly long. In this particular case, the poor soul had to wait for nine long days to get his number. Even after this, he found it very difficult to get a footing, so to say, in the Court's trial place for eight days. The cases of souls of higher planes were conducted and after that the cases of souls of the fourth plane were taken up. Even then his rank was somewhere near two hundred. In a day about 20 normal cases are disposed of and at this rate it took therefore some 10 days more. After this delay of about one month his trial began.

Protracted Trial

After all these preliminaries, the name of the soul is called out and he is brought forward by the spirit-in-charge to, we may say, the cage. If the soul concerned has some relations or friends who can further his case, they are asked to go to the witness box. If the soul was a known man, the group of philanthropist pleaders think over the soul's case and if they think it necessary to plead, they request Yama to grant permission to them for the purpose; and Yama at once decides one way or the other whether to grant the request or not. In this particular case, the soul had many friends and was therefore asked to select ten spirits to represent him at the trial.

Further details of the trial will be taken up subsequently. It is desirable here to understand how the trial is protracted and lengthened. Even after the above mentioned preliminaries are gone through, the trial does not commence at once, since the Yama orders spirits who are in the Investigation Department of the Court to collect all relevant facts about the soul who is undergoing trial. This investigation takes some time; in some cases, it requires a couple of days. After that, the reading of the records is ordered. Many other items are next taken in hand and Yama then gives his judgment which appears like a sermon, as it is couched in moralising terms and sounds like an exhortation. It may be perhaps argued that such delays are common enough in the ordinary courts of the Earth and that there should be no reason to grumble about it. But in view of the fact that spirits take practically no time to perform any act, it should be admitted that so much delay is not justifiable and some speedy means of conducting trials at the divine courts should be devised.

Detailed Investigation and Procedure at the Court

There is a very well developed Investigation Department under the Court's control and supervision, and many intelligent spirits find in it good scope for their ability. As soon as Yama orders an investigation to be conducted, the head of this department sends out three spirits. One goes to the record keeper and takes out as much material as possible about the soul for the records. The second spirit goes to the world below with an elemental to get proper information about the soul's actions during the last birth. It may seem rather queer that a good spirit should form an alliance with a distinctly baser soul. But, as we have already observed, spirits have no physical powers and it would not be feasible for them to carry on an investigation without such help. Why should such elementals help in this matter was a point undisclosed to me for a long time. Recently however I had to mix with such an elemental and he explained to me that he got absolute freedom in return for service thus rendered to the Court. These two spirits therefore go to the place where the soul concerned used to live. The elemental would enter into a living person's body and make him talk with persons who knew many things about that soul. In most cases, it is not so easy to enter into someone's body; and it takes a long time before this can be accomplished. The elemental gives all the information he has gathered to the other spirit and they discuss the points involved therein. Very often, they do not agree and the differences between them are responsible for some further unnecessary delay in the commencement and conduct of the trial. In this manner at any rate the spirit who has gone to the world is able to secure all necessary information about the soul.

At this stage, it is necessary to give some idea of the topics which are included in the investigation. Yama requires information on the following points:

In the first instance, it is necessary to know whether the person had a normal end or whether the end was due to some abnormal cause. Here it should be made clear that a death caused by bodily ailment or disease constitutes a normal death, but if there was no such disease and if the death was caused by, say, mental weakness taking the form of an accident, it constitutes an abnormal end. Deaths due to suicide and murders, stand in a class by themselves. In case of a normal death there is a very little to investigate; but suicides and murders means a lot of trouble to the investigators. The murderer has to be found out and his name has to be recorded.

Analysis of Human Actions

Besides this, here is another point that needs analysis and investigation. The spirits have to make a classified list of the actions of the soul under trial which were good and those which were evil. There is a further classification of deeds into those which were done to benefit his own self and those that were meant to benefit others.

Men during their lifetime perform so many actions that a classification is not an easy task. But to make an attempt is the only thing possible. 'good deeds' are composed in the first place of 'honest beliefs' and 'honest actions'. In some cases, it is difficult to define honesty and class an action as honest; hence the use of the word beliefs. There are very few persons who can be strictly considered honest and the investigating spirit is therefore instructed to be lenient in his investigation of certain actions. Another important good action is the performance 'of duty'. It can be safely asserted that duty is one of the most important factors in Yama's code of good actions. Those persons who are able to do their duty towards themselves and their families are said to have used their tenure of life in a most suitable manner. Some people go a stage further in their pursuit of the religion of duty, and I am sure, they merit the favour of Yama. 'Good conduct' of course adds to one's spiritual and material advancement, though strangely enough it is given a lesser weight than the performance of duty. Sometimes a man whose conduct is not as good as it ought to be gets on successfully, if he has done his duty. It is known all over the world that if you help others, God helps you, and some help rendered to others will always stand in good stead to the person who had the foresight to do so. This in general, should in my view be the classification to be adopted while reviewing good deeds by the spirits who investigate.

Coming to 'bad actions' or the darker side of humanity as such, a 'wilful wrong' done to others forms one of the most wicked actions which make the souls who perform such deeds liable to severe punishment. Next in magnitude come the deeds which are certainly bad but are not the result of any predetermined thought and therefore such 'unpremeditated bad deeds' to some extent are pardonable of liable to lighter punishment only. Then we come to 'dishonesty' which is a most common vice among people who are less fortunately placed, being on the lower rungs of the financial ladder. In cases of hand-to-mouth existence, such dishonesty is to a large extent permissible though it is never encouraged. Bad conduct is severely dealt with if such misdeeds are not counter-balanced by some good actions.

In this manner the investigators accumulate all necessary information and return to the spirit world.

The elemental of course goes to his own plane, while the spirit goes to the Investigation Department, and reports all the facts to the Head of the Department.

By this time the spirit who had gone to the record keeper has also returned and makes a statement to that effect.

A third spirit is now asked to go through all those reports and then to consult the soul about it. He should incorporate only those items which receive the consent of the soul concerned. In his recorded report he should make some remarks about the points on which there is a divergence of opinion between the principal investigator and the soul. From this it should be pretty clear that all this takes a long time to be ready for presentation before the Court.

Now I come to the actual procedure at the Court.

The soul is just before Yama and the trial begins when the Court is informed that the investigation is at an end. A call made and there comes the prosecutor to open the case. This spirit is not supposed to go through the information received but he is only asked to state the facts revealed by the record which was made when the soul had parted from his body. His remarks are rather general and vague. This statement only serves the purpose of putting Yama into touch with the soul concerned. After this is over, the spirit from the Investigation Department comes forward with the information collected. He in the first instance gives details about death and discusses how far such an end was normal. After devoting a long time to this topic, he begins to scan the list of good deeds. Acts which were done for his own good are taken up first. A note is made of such good acts by a spirit whose duty is to record the proceedings of all cases. The spirit of the Investigation Department always gives explanations and reasons for considering some acts as good or normal as the case may be. Very often it so happens that an act considered good by the spirit may be classed as normal by Yama. It hardly needs telling you that Yama's view is final and binding. The spirit next comes to deeds which are good but which are done for others.

Controversy often arises on the point where a particular act may be said to be performed for others. In case of people who believe in the joint family system, the concept of the family being broader than the normal idea of a family, most acts are not included in the group we are discussing. The underlying idea is that those acts only which were done for persons beyond the family circle should come under this class. In this respect the Hindus are at a considerable disadvantage as from very old times their idea of a family is quite different from the ideas of other nations. After the good side in the list has been analysed and presented, we find that Yama orders the spirit to stop and asks the soul concerned to give his view in a sentence. He has to agree or disagree only and not to argue. In most cases, the position is made so clear that the soul has no other option but to agree entirely. After this is done, the spirit again resumes his discussion, dealing with the darker side of the particular side. Wilful acts are discussed first and in respect of every such wilful bad deed, Yama makes the soul agree with him. Of Course, every detail is all the while recorded by the spirit-in-charge. After the scrutiny of wilful acts, there comes the class of acts which are bad but more or less accidental in nature. Acts, not backed by a motive, are to some extent pardonable and hence put in a different class by Yama. In such deeds the consent of the soul is not sought, for these deeds are not to be given prime importance. The investigating spirit, having now finished his survey of the soul's actions, takes Yama's leave which is granted in normal circumstances. Yama now requests the honorary pleaders to speak on behalf of the soul. This is not always allowed as we have seen before. It is only in case where the soul has achieved a certain status, that this privilege is granted. Assuming that it is granted, it depends on the will of the pleaders to plead or not. They are requested not to speak on all the deeds but only on such topics have not received full attention or which have been totally ignored. Furthermore, they can speak on the classification and often about deeds which are on the border line. They can throw doubts on the charges levelled against the soul and in a general way give an idea of the soul's character and achievements. In conclusion they can even plead for mercy to Yama. This in a way completes the major part of the proceedings, barring Yama's decision in consultation with his Councillors.

No Defence

It must have appeared to my readers that so far I have been speaking of the official conduct of the cases; but I have not neglected the other side, the defendant, the soul. The fact is that the soul is never asked to give any views of his own nor to express disagreement or doubt the opinions expressed by officials of the highest court. As has been seen before, the soul is only asked to agree or disagree when expressly desired by Yama. It must be therefore pretty clear to you that, all through, the soul plays a passive part in the long-drawn proceedings. It may successfully be argued that without hearing both the sides, no decision can be correct and just. This is correct in case of the imperfect human agency; but in this divine tribunal, the agency employed is certainly superhuman if not divine. I, for one, believe that it is good not to mix up the views of the higher agency with those of the soul which is of an absolutely different class. The human conception of justice is in most cases rather more lenient than the conception which Yama has and this it is which very often dissatisfies most souls, who are not adjudged as fit for promotion to a higher plane. But it is agreed on all hands that Yama wants to maintain a high standard of justice which explains his unpopularity among the lower orders of spirits and souls.

The Ruling

After all that was to be investigated has been put forward by the officials and the honorary pleaders, Yama begins his speech or sermon whichever you choose to call it. In the first instance, he expresses his regret for causing delay and the resultant hardship. He then congratulates the soul for his good deeds and devotes some time over good deeds done for others. This part of his speech makes the soul feel that Yama Raja has a soft corner for him, little knowing that the remaining part is a caustic sermon. Then Yama comes to the darker side of his life. For accidental bad deeds he merely warns the soul, the warning being couched in more or less mild terms. Bad acts which were done wilfully are examined by him in full details and he makes sure that the soul realises the enormity of his misdeeds. In case the soul does not realise it, Yama asks the soul to justify his contention with proper proofs. In such rare cases only does Yama himself cross-examine the obstinate soul. So far he has only examined the facts of the case. But now, he comes to the critical part of his decision. In the beginning he explains the doctrine of good acts counter-balancing bad deeds and then tells him that in his case there is either an excess of good deeds over bad ones or the contrary. If the good deeds out-number the bad, he assumes that the soul is properly trained up and therefore he need not be detained any longer; but if the excess is the other way, he gets wild with rage and he begins to advise, scold, reproach or denounce the soul as strongly as possible. The soul who is hearing Yama gets frightened and invariably requests Yama to pardon his short-comings and misdeeds. But the god having assumed a wild form refuses to hear anything and proceeds to give his final judgment. Honorary pleaders can help the soul as they have the power to ask Yama to give his decision the next day. Assuming that the soul concerned had an excess of good deeds, Yama states: "Mr. X has lived his tenure of life successfully and has not proved a burden to mankind, but has in a small measure helped others over and above securing a fund of happiness for himself and his family. He should be lifted from his present plane and be posted in a higher plane as reward for his fruitful existence. His unison should take place on 21st day from today; he should come to the Court next week for getting a permit for a new birth." In the other case, in which the bad deeds predominate over good ones, the following would be the contents of the decision: "Mr. X, has wasted all the time allotted to him to show his worth and in a general way has proved a burden to his relations and friends, nay to the whole society. His conduct has proved to be far from satisfactory; he has allowed good opportunities to slip away and therefore he should suffer for his actions. The Court does not desire to penalise him, but it only orders him to remain in the old plane and it is necessary that a better use of the new birth should be made. The soul should present himself after 41 days for a new birth permit."

Assignment of Planes

The Court is said to have fulfilled when the decision is given by the Yama in council. After that, the assignment of planes is made by the Assignment Department which is controlled by Yama. The soul should, as soon as possible, go there and inform them clearly of the decision given. The spirit-in-charge refers to the records of decisions and then gives the name and number of the plane assigned to the soul. He also sends a spirit to show the plane to the soul so that he may find it easy to reach there. He is then asked to return in a reasonably short time as he is not supposed to stay there before unison and the new birth permit is required as a sort of an entrance pass.

New Birth Order

After the lapse of the necessary period, the soul presents himself to the Court for a new birth order. As usual, it takes some time before Yama can give attention to the tired soul. Furthermore, even when Yama attends to him, he has to inform the Creator about it as it is. He who has to provide for him. After the necessary information is obtained, and after it is ascertained that provision can be made, Yama asks the soul to choose from certain specified types of births. He however gives no guarantee of giving the birth selected by him. Very often, the option given is such that is tends to become a Hobson's choice. The riddle often is incapable of solution and therefore Yama gives plenty of time to the soul to decide; even consulting people of the world through mediums is allowed. The idea is that Yama does not want to bear the odium of having given a bad birth. Somehow or other, the selection is made and it is now for Yama to approve of it or force on him birth which in his opinion is appropriate. In very many cases, Yama agrees but there seems to be no definite basis on which he decides this problem. In my talk with him, he revealed that approval of a soul's choice is a reward for his good conduct at the Court.

Interval between Successive Births

It may be observed that rebirth does not necessarily take place at once. In normal cases, a year elapses between death and the new birth. It must be made clear however that there are instances in which souls have not been given a new birth for years together. The rules which govern the determination of this interval are quite unknown; but it appears that, in case a suitable birth is not found, the matter may be left over and arrears are in that case disposed of after some years. Further, it may happen that the soul may be progressing very slowly and even though it is not fit enough for salvation, it requires some long rest and rebirth may be consequently delayed.

Unison

Ordering of a new birth marks the completion of the proceedings at the Court, and it is thought fit by Yama at this juncture to allow the soul to be united with his spirit-identity for the period during which the soul has to wait, as rebirth does not take place at once. The spirit of the soul is asked to come down to Yama's region and as it is the will of Yama, the soul and the spirit get united into a greater soul. He feels much happier than before by being in touch with his counterpart after a lapse of say fifty to sixty years. Unison is in a way a normal incident; but rare as such incidents are, they tend to be abnormal. After this happens, the spirit is made to forget his past life so that he may take more interest in the soul's latest life. It may be observed that a spirit can at the most be expected to remember only a few incidents of his past life, and that too for one birth. After this unison, the greater soul is entitled to occupy his plane for a short time. This concludes our survey of the progress of the soul through Yama's Court. In the next chapter we shall see him in his plane forming an integral part of the same.

Qualities Needed for Progress

If the reader has carefully followed the preceding pages, he must have gathered that the qualities which help us in the world of the living also help us to weather the storms of the trial more easily. Divine concepts of good qualities are in a general sense the same as the human conception of such virtues. In India it is believed that idol worship helps one's soul to achieve progress; but it may be stated here that such worship bears no fruits except that it may prove a sort of a check on certain baser desires having sway over the reason of such persons. The chief factor which leads to spiritual and material advancement of souls is the standard of duty which has developed in a particular soul. The higher the standard of duty maintained, the larger is the reward reserved for that soul. The concept of DUTY is not only an important factor, but broadly speaking it is the only factor which helps one in his spiritual march towards salvation. It is said that in very old times many advanced souls used to leave worldly connections and confine themselves in some lonely place for their spiritual advancement; but if I may be permitted to express my opinion, I must state that those souls have not made use of their surroundings; but, having gone out of their world, they only made their life of such a nature that important problems which face others do not harass them. They have thus shirked the burden of duty and the reward is reduced to that extent. It should not be misunderstood that other good actions have no effect, as all things great and small have a gradual and cumulative efffect, in deciding the usefulness or otherwise of a being's existence.

Special Treatment: Mediums and Instruments

So far we have spoken of normal cases. I must acknowledge that there are no prejudices or predilections in Yama's Court; but in some cases, certain privileges are granted to souls awaiting their trial if they have rendered some useful service. This mode of tempering justice with mercy is in no way a reflection on Yama's impartiality. The special treatment is a well earned reward after many years of work in the field of spiritualism. Mediums, who are not frauds, are treated with mercy but no special help is given as regards their spiritual advancement. But mediums who are not only genuine but also have not turned their abilities into professional channels are held in esteem by the Court, and in giving the decision, some help is given either in the shape of reduction of punishment or in giving a better plane with a suitable birth, which would give them further opportunities to reveal more about the unknown or misunderstood world of spirits. Instruments however receive no benefits or special treatment since they aer held to have helped their mediums only and not the authorities. I may, therefore, give a hint to would-be spiritualists that if at all they take up spiritualism, they should do it without any idea of reward. Let them have the ideal of service to humanity and despise the idea of any personal gain; otherwise disappointment will be in store for them.

CHAPTER IV

THE SEVEN STAGES OR PLANES

Location — Presiding Deities.

First Plane : The Patala — Is it Hell? — The Court — Elementals — Activity of Spirits — Haunting.

Second Plane : The Bhu Loka — Spirits of Low Order — No Activity — Freedom from Control.

Third Plane : The Tapa Loka — Spirits of Middle Class — Control — Attendance at Trials — Collective Actions — Touch with the World.

Fourth Plane : The Chandra Loka — Contented Spirits — Freedom to Move — Touch with Higher.Powers — Yama's Visits.

Fifth Plane : The Surya Loka — Ambitious Spirits — Administrative Work — Energiser — Presiding Deity.

Sixth Plane : The Swarga Loka — Happy Souls — Cold Spirits — Loss of Touch with the World — Loss of Memory.

Seventh Plane : The Deva Loka — God-like Souls — No Touch with Mediums — No Activity — Rest.

Location

So far we have spoken of the spirits and their life at the Court. In this chapter other phases of the lfie of spirits will be taken up. It is at least well known in India that the world of spirits is divided into seven planes the western world too, the idea of such planes or stage is becoming current. The man in the world of the living does not know for certain the number planes in the spirit-world; and very often speculation is rife in that matter. Sofaras I know however there are only seven stages, created for spirits of all types. Even accepting this fact, there is further much difficulty, about naming these planes or stages. In view of the fact that no official names exist, the best way is to allocate numbers to these stages. But, I have come across

Indian names for these stages and for the purpose of this book, I have selected seven names which incidentally indicate the nature of each plane.

Each of these planes is just an expanse of space like Yama's Court. The different stages have an area according to their needs. In distributing space, the higher plane is given a smaller area than the lower plane, because there are always fewer spirits in such stages. It is just like having more third class carriages and few upper class ones in a railway train. These areas are just a few hundred miles from the living world on the outer border of the atmosphere. It hardly needs any reiteration that spirits do not require any thing like the earth to support them in space. They live in space and can move on any part of the world. But they cannot move over any higher plane than the one allotted to them in the spirit world.

Presiding Deities

It is a very natural question to ask about the arrangement for controlling spirits who reside in these planes. A very elaborate system for control is devised to meet this primary need. Every plane or 'loka' has its own 'deity', who is entrusted with the work of controlling spirits in general and making it practicable for spirits in administrative departments to control them. If there is any mismanagement, the deity in charge will be held responsible. The rules of control are not the same in all lokas; they vary to a large extent. In some stages, the control is nominal; in others it is pronounced, and in others still, complete. The principles which decide the extent of the control will be dealt with when we come to a detailed analysis of those stages. There is some conflict of opinion amongst us about the term 'deity' and I in my memorandum submitted to Yama Raj, suggested the word, spirit-control. As usual, however, he was not prepared to accept the suggestion; but only very recently he uses the word, while using the English language. It may be pointed out here that the language spoken depends upon the language of the spirit concerned, and higher spirits are expected to master all important languages.

We shall now commence a detailed analysis of these different planes.

FIRST PLANE—THE PATALA

The Patala

The first 'loka' is known as the 'patala'. The word signifies the lower regions and it is in fact a region for spirits of inferior calibre. Some may imagine it to be a physically lower plane; but that idea is wrong altogether as all planes are more or less only a few hundred miles away from the earth. It should be noted that the Patala is not the world of Satan but an integral part of the whole spirit world. In this region, there are two broad divisions one forming the Yama's Court and the other, the real 'patala'. It is this part which is meant for spirits of a low order. In the other part, all souls have to go for their trial and to that extent, it is not a real visit to Patala or to the first plane. To my mind, the Court is absolutely a different stage, but it is accidentally merged into the Patala Loka.

It may appear strange to some persons that Yama should create such a hybrid plane and a few years back, I also shared that view. But now as I have come in touch with the internal organisation of Yama's Court, I can safely assert that it is so mixed up in order to get the advantage of the lower spirits in the work of investigation while conducting cases in the Court. The mixing up, though accidental, is thus to a certain extent desirable, and these two absolutely different types of planes form one of the most important regions in the spirit world.

Is It Hell ?

Patala Loka to an Indian mind is a plane associated with something unpalatable in its atmosphere. Even among the English people, they regard such a region as belonging to Satan. There is a belief that it is the region reserved for the worst type of souls. It is rather strange to find such a belief current among Indians in particular. If an Indian or better still a Hindu comes to know that his relative is in Patala, he feels as if that person's soul is transferred to Hell, a region of trouble and oppression. But to remove the misconception, I would like to state that no HELL whatsoever exists in the spirit world. But, after all, Hell is relative term and though we may term the first Plane as Patala to distinguish at from Hell, the first plane is the worst stage to which a soul can be sent and to that extent it may very broadly be regarded as a kind of Hell.

The Court

We have in the preceding chapter spoken of the Court as far as the subject of trial was concerned. It is now desirable to give an idea of the Court not as the Divine Tribunal but as a Plane in the spirit world. It has about the same area as the other planes; but the peculiarity of this region lies in the fact that there are no permanent residents and all those who come go away, as soon as their trial is over. It does not thus have the appearance of an ordinary plane; but it has that office- look which is completely absent in other planes. The number of officials who frequent this plane is also large. The importance of this plane cannot be denied as it is also the centre of the Administration Department of the spirit world. A detailed review of this department will be taken up later on, as it has no direct bearing on this chapter.

Elementals

There are two broad classes into which the spirits residing in the Patala Loka can be divided. In the first class come spirits of the ordinary type. These spirits have usually an inferior brain power and they are in this plane only on that account. All of them are, in my esteem, good people and I do not know why they should suffer because they have a poor brain. Is it not the mistake of the Creator* to have brought such souls into existence? At any rate, once created, they should be given favorable treatment and there should be some device to

* As it appeared to me a great presumption to criticise the Creator, here as also later on, I always made it a point to draw Sir Arthur's attention and to ask him whether he would not like to modify the sentence. But he was firm and would not give up the position he had taken up, and as the book was his work, I have retained such passages, as dictated.

improve their lot. The other class consists of spirits who have very powerful and fertile brains; but the only trouble with them is that the power was misdirected and they reaped the fruits of their actions by being assigned to Patala Loka. These spirits are very intelligent and have a creative genius, but all such power has been used for bad deeds. Being base souls, they are called elementals. These intelligent spirits who use their abilities in such a wrong way, are not able to proceed any further; they have to stay in this region long as they continue to act in the same wicked manner. Spirits with a very low order of brain are also called elementals; but, to my mind they should not be so called because the word 'elemental' has a bad odour about it, insofar as it suggests wilful wickedness or misdemeanour on the part of the spirits concerned.

Activity of Spirits

In every plane, spirits reside, but their activities are very often quite different and a study of their activities in different planes is desirable. But we will here confine ourselves to the activities of elementals only.

Elementals who have not brains are by their very nature dull and usually not ready to do any work even when they were in their physical existence. While alive, they are more or less idle and are in a way dependent on others and thus obviate the need for supporting themselves. In the spirit world too, they never move out of their dens as it were and they have made it a point not to attend the Court. If they attended it, it would help them to progress further; but little as their minds work, they do not realise their own interests. Such spirits do not like to go to mediums even, as they are very often not called by them and even when called, they fail to give any good account of themselves on the Board. Some however maintain that if the mediums used automatic writing, these spirits are able to manage much better; but I personally hold that whatever the mode of invoking them, they fail to satisfy the person concerned. They only move about in their plane and are quite harmless to living beings and other spirits. They have not got the power to haunt and therefore are not at all in a position to harm others.

Now coming to the second class of elementals, they are endowed with very strong mental powers, and their abilities are much greater than those of the spirits in the other planes. Furthermore, they have some peculiar force in them which is usually absent in others. This force is of such a nature that it serves the needs of physical energy, and it is because of this force that they are able to do substantial work which others cannot do. They always like to 'go to mediums' provided they find the same base nature in them which they themselves possess. If a good hearted medium were to call such a spirit, perhaps he may not come at all and even if he came he would not like the medium. Good mediums and spiritualists do not therefore usually come in contact with elementals and some of them on that account very often doubt the existence of the elementals altogether. All elementals are however very keen to keep themselves in touch with the happenings in the world through their mediums. Their second activity is called 'service to the court' because, a large number of elementals are employed in the investigation of all the cases that are before the Court. It may appear rather strange that the divine court should employ the agency of elementals who are base and not worthy of performing such duties. It has been put forward by some responsible officers of Yama's Court that good spirits have not got the necessary power of carrying on the work of investigation themselves. It requires spirits of higher calibre and such spirits can be easily found among the elementals. It may be argued perhaps that the spirits with good brains can be found in the sixth and the seventh planes; but it may be pointed out that their powers are nominal and useless for the work in view. In this work the elemental proves very useful indeed to the Court. It is with his help that the administration of justice becomes possible. If the elementals are faithful in discharging their duties, they are given some reward either in the shape of a good birth or in the shape of giving a post in the administrative department: but in no case, is a higher plane assigned to them. That can be done only if the base nature has improved even to a very small extent. This activity however does not full occupy all the elementals and master brains something more to do.

Haunting

A large number of intelligent spirits of this plane therefore indulge in an activity called 'haunting'. This term is not a happy one insofar as it does not give a correct idea of such activities. But even after long deliberation I have failed to find a better word than 'haunting'. There are two broad divisions of this type of actions. In one class, the spirits concerned do not materialise, but carry on their work through their mediums. Such haunting is to a large extent harmless, though cases have been found where such haunting has resulted in actual harassment. Thus a spirit, while talking on the Board, gives some threat to the medium or his client, and very often such threats so impress themselves on the mind of the medium that the spirit is successful in getting his desires fulfilled. Thus I know of a case, in which a medium was compelled to kill a certain person only because his spirit asked him to do so under the threat of death. Sometimes elementals, who are fond of talking and arguing, impersonate certain spirits or are even bold enough to disclose their name and make the medium talk with them If on any ground such talks are discouraged, they employ threats. It may be contended that those threats if ignored would not materialise, but such contention is wrong because the elementals have larger powers as regards materialisation than other spirits. This leads us to the second type of haunting where elementals resort to materialisation. The spirit usually has one medium and both of them have established very cordial relations to their mutual advantage. Such mediums do not use any of the modes of invoking spirits mentioned in a previous chapter. They have such an elemental under their clutches, though this subjection usually involves a lot of trouble and waiting; but once the relationship is established, the spirit becomes very tame and acts as a tool for the medium. Thus, many base acts are done through the instrumentality of the elemental and those who suffer from the mischievous pranks played by an elemental consider it as haunting. They may think that the spirit is unnecessarily troubling them, little knowing that the spirit is unnecessarily troubling them, little knowing that the spirit, being a tool, acts according to the wishes of his medium. But a natural question—What benefit would the elemental derive from being a tool of such a medium? The problem was difficult of solution to some of my friends and to me; but, as I came into contact with an important elemental, he told me that if there was no work, there could be no elementals, as they always required some food for their brains. If they cannot find any work, they prefer to act as tools rather than idle away their time. The philosophy of the elementals is thus worth appreciating, but, the only drawback is that they misdirect their energies.

This plane is in a way a place where there is some thing more than democracy, as no government exists for them. Yet, Yama Raj usually keeps himself in touch with the happenings in this corner of the spirit-world.

SECOND PLANE — THE BHU LOKA

The Bhu Loka

From Patala, we come to the Bhu Loka or the second plane in the spirit world. It may be mentioned here that these planes are near each other and there is little change of atmosphere except in the Patala. This region is called Bhu Loka and that too for a good reason. Spirits who are assigned to this plane are full of earthly desire and, if not all, most of them are dominated by the influence of the baser instincts of mankind. It should not be understood however from this that all who have the fortune or misfortune to stay here are wicked, because after all one factor does not decide a case.

Spirits of Low Order

These general remarks do not convey the real type of these spirits and their qualities. In the first place, many of them are below the average, so far as the measure of their intelligence is concerned. Some of them have even not the capacity to do any act which can be regarded as substantial; others, who possess some powers, are bent upon enjoying all through and lead a useless existence and in my opinion are a burden to humanity. Then, there are those, who are fairly clever and are able to put in some work, but who refuse to do anything except certain things, which satisfy their baser instincts. Such is the state of Bhu Loka. The last type of spirits are a danger to the spirit-world and their bodies on the Earth are a striking monument of passion.

No Activity

In a general way we have glanced through the personnel with which we are concerned at present. The natural desire of an investigator would be to get an idea of their activities, and I should also give a natural reply. I should ask him a question. What would such a person do on Earth? He would certainly lead a life without any activity if he could get his bread somehow or other. Such spirits never care about the administration of the spirit-world nor do they go to hear trials, which are otherwise popular with spirits of other planes. The chief reason is that they have never thought of progress in their lives. Most of them prefer to do nothing rather than go to hear trials, much less to do any active work in the Court, or an other department. There is one thing which would interest them, but as that desire or passion cannot be satisfied in the spirit-world, they are very often restless. They would like to be called by mediums if they can find in them some satisfaction of their desire. I suppose you have not been able to call such spirits, because their company is bound to have some undesirable influence on all who come in contact with them.

Freedom from Control

The ways of the spirit-world and different from those of the world of the living and the method of administration in this loka is a case in point. Those spirits, who have not got a developed sense of responsibility, are given up as incorrigible. I had a discussion with Yama himself and he agreed that some means to improve them were necessary but he held that certain means were already in force at the present moment to achieve the purpose; I have however failed to find any such means in force. To my utter amazement, he told me that they have a control in the shape of bitter experience and bad rebirths. He was further of opinion that they showed some improvement only when they learnt by actual experience. The divine authorities have thus thought it fit to let them exist it without practically any control, and allow them to do as they pleased. But one thing more and that is that Shree Laxmidevi or the Goddess of Wealth is supposed to look after this plane in a general way, though she is strictly forbidden to control any spirit under any circumstances. From my experience, however, I can say with confidence that her presence in this loka is to a great extent responsible for making good spirits out of bad.

The Yama in Council has decided that spirits on the border line should not be assigned to this plane, because the company of other spirits makes it impossible for them to improve and the chances of being dragged lower are many. This ruling is responsible for the sparse population there.

THIRD PLANE — THE TAPA LOKA

The Tapa Loka

We now leave behind the lower strata of society in the spirit world. We do not yet jump over however to the cream, but we come to the typical middle class. This region which is just near the Bhu Loka is called the Tapa Loka. TAPA in popular parlance means penance and to some, it may appear that it is not a suitable name because there is no relation between tapa and the spirits of this stage. But, let me remove the illusion; the word "TAPA" is used in the sense of good natured. It is certainly true that people in this plane are much better then those in the previous two lokas described above. Furthermore, this loka is famous for its system and method. Every activity is perfectly organised and well managed. I, for one, believe that this plane is most suitable for a person who loves an active and useful life and we very often find some very intelligent persons in this loka.

Spirits of Middle Class

So far we had a hurried bird's eye view of the plane in general. We shall now take up the detailed analysis of some interesting features which are important for our purpose. Most of the spirits who come hear or rather who are assigned to this plane are of the middle class. But middle class, according to what standard? I feel there are no hard and fast rules about it and the only way to get an idea of such a variable standard is to study a few lives of spirits who are found in this stage. At this stage it is not desirable to enter into a lengthy discussion about such cases; but if my readers have any faith in my judgment, I may state that there are three factors viz. character, capital and capacity, which go a long way in deciding a case. The authorities are always inclined to put most souls in this class and that is why we find the largest number of spirits in this plane. When deciding, it is very easy to class a soul middle-class by asserting that one or the other of the three factors is absent or not properly developed. To some it may appear that the world consists of many souls who would be classed in this group; but I feel if only one of these three qualities is taken into consideration, the number of such spirits would be fairly small. As it is, I think, it is a faulty method of judging persons, because it is very rare that such a combination of three attributes can be found. But divine methods are also very rigid like those of governments in the world of the living and it is no use finding fault with it. I very often wonder whether God or Creator feels ashamed at finding so many of His products turning out to be merely mediocre. If I were in His position, I would certainly feel ashamed. However, it is no business of mine to cast any reflections upon such a Being.

Control

We have seen that a vast majority of spirits are forced to live in this plane. Naturally the problem of administration is also complex. The spirits of this plane are usually of a good nature and most of them are well behaved. The rules for them are not rigid and only exceptional cases are under strict control. These spirits are allowed to go to good mediums, and whenever they go to a new medium they are enjoined to report the fact to their head-spirit who is responsible for every 100 spirits. Further they should return home before 12 midnight. In case they fail to do so, adequate reasons have to be given without any demand being made by their head. These are the main points as regards control and supervision. So far as the official reports go, the conduct of the majority is more than satisfactory. Yama thinks that this region does not require a strong control and this work is therefore assigned to the Goddess of Learning or to put it in the Indian fashion, Shree Saraswati Devi. She is a goddess with a marked personality and a strong driving force. She is able to control the whole plane very well and yet maintain extremely cordial relations with most of the souls entrusted to her care. Her kindness is also worthy of note, insofar as she tries to promote many spirits to a higher plane by being liberal as regards the attribute of intelligence.

Attendance at Trials

Devi Shree Saraswati always makes it a point to impress the importance of hearing trials upon every new recruit individually. As we have remarked somewhere previously in this book, this idea of hearing trials is appreciated by the authorities in particular. To add to this, many spirits of this loka are themselves very keen on hearing trials, as they went to improve their lot by getting some good out of it. When I died, as Arthur, and came to the spirit world, this idea did not appeal to me on various grounds. But after a few years' stay, I feel that in the absence of any other agency to impart knowledge, hearing of trials was the only method available for self-improvement. I suggested that, if some sort of a school could be started, the purpose would be served in a much shorter space of time, because, after all, trials are unduly long and tiresome. But the reply I received was quite appropriate because it contained the following sentence:

"Your idea is based on a misconception insofar as the Court trials are designed to keep the spirits engaged for a much longer time than it is possible to do in a school. Too much leisure is not desirable."

Collective Actions

If I may be permitted to make a sort of a sweeping statement, mediocre people are never sure of themselves and would always flock together. They can do things properly if somebody leads them, as they lack the essential quality of leadership. These remarks are designed to justify their attitude of collective actions. I have even seen spirits who take with them a score more, even when they go to a medium and when asked questions by the audience, they consult each other. When some big problem confronts them, they cannot decide for themselves. In a way I appreciate their method because after all, a larger number of poor brains can find out some way out of the wood when an isolated brain fails to make any headway.

Touch with the World

MAYA or worldly desires are things difficult to conquer and we know of cases where people who have renounced the world often become victims of such an irresistible lure. Some people are the easy prey of these worldly desires and even when they die, unfulfilled desires dominate their life in the next world too. If a minute analysis were made in various planes it would be apparent that people of the Tapa Loka are invariably keen on maintaining a strong contact with the world, which they like most. Thus weaker mediums would always find that it is very easy to establish contact with them insofar as very strong co-operation is exhibited by spirits. I myself am in favour of such an attitude on the part of spirits; but those who are particularly successful in the World of the Dead are of opinion that such attachment on their part is detrimental to their own interests. I however fail to agree; because if they talk or make merry with the living, it should add to their efficiency and influence their conduct. More particulalry spirits in the administrative department might well be in touch with the world if they have reliable mediums. "Reliable" is a word which created dispute among some officials, but I prefer to be mute on the point. Some are inclined to believe that it is a most unfriendly act to call spirits whom we know; but whatever may be the arguments, I feel invoking them does not drag them down. Perhaps the chances are just the other way.

FOURTH PLANE — THE CHANDRA LOKA

The Chandra Loka

Chandra means the "moon" and the name is particularly suitable, insofar as it gives an idea of calmness which is so characteristic of the Moon's light. This 'loka' is just near the 'tapa loka' and it is large enough to make the existence of spirits more comfortable than in other lower planes. One may ask why? We have already left behind the middle class and we are in the midst of the upper strata of spirits and naturally they get better treatment. The density of population is much smaller here than in the preceding 'lokas' because it is very difficult to cross the cordon of the middle class. Only those who are extremely fortunate do not stagnate in the Tapa Loka. Some spirits feel that the conditions of this loka are so tempting that one would like to remain in this plane for ever. Even I agree to a certain extent, because the only serious drawback is that the 'whole' atmosphere is incompatible with the cherishing of any ambition.

Contented Spirits

To come to the characteristics of the spirits of this 'loka', the most striking one is their contented nature. Somehow or other, as soon as a spirit is promoted from a lower plane to this plane, he gets such an amount of satisfaction that it kills his desires completely. I do not know why they should be satisfied so soon. When they are in the third plane, they perpetually grumble about bad treatment and particularly about the whole administrative machinery; but soon after their grievances are redressed, they begin to admire it, while people like me would never get complete satisfaction and would always have some grievances and complaints to make. Some persons have always shown their inclination towards contentment and in the opinion of the authorities, such persons are regarded as worthy of further promotion and good rebirth.

Freedom to Move

In this LOKA, people are very quiet and calm and therefore there is an absence of any elaborate system of regulations. Chandra Loka spirits are allowed complete freedom of movement and they are at liberty to go to their mediums any time they choose. In this respect, this loka compares very favourably with the third plane. It may be pointed out that no misuse of such liberty is allowed and be it said to the credit of the spirits too, that most of them give a satisfactory account of their conduct. I have met spirits from this plane who are so fond of their mediums on the Earth that they sometimes stay with them for some days. Such an action would be seriously dealt with in other planes; but here no notice is taken of it.

Touch with Higher Powers

It has been remarked more than once that the general culture and circumstances of the spirits here are much better than can be expected in lower planes. Naturally spirits with better powers of reasoning are in a position to take more care about their personal matters. But as we know, the sources of information regarding advancement, both spiritually and materially, are not confined to this loka. Therefore, intelligent spirits always make it a point to be in touch with souls who have been particularly successful in the two worlds. 'Higher Powers' do not mean divine powers, but only spirits who have achieved something which can be called substantial. It may be further added that such contact is easy to establish because higher spirits are always eager to ameliorate the condition and solve the troubles of others.

Yama's Visits

The problem of control is non-existent in this plane, and as a matter of fact it is nobody's region. But, after all, even good spirits might raise some issues and therefore, some presiding god has been deemed desirable. But those who worked there, being fond of ruling, created much unrest and since the last 10,000 years, Yama has removed Kalika or the Goddess of Destruction, and he himself goes to Chandra Loka, not regularly but pretty often. He has won the admiration of the calm and quiet spirits by his clear-cut methods of doing business. When we were talking of the Court, we often remarked about the Yama Raj being a strict and impartial judge; but he is here in a different form altogether. He looks all the more merciful and invariably tempers justice with mercy. One may well ponder over this change of mood, but the reason is not far to seek; in the former case, he is a judge, while in the latter, he is to look after the spirits who are entrusted to his care and naturally there is a change in his angle of vision.

FIFTH PLANE — THE SURYA LOKA

The Surya Loka

The history of this plane is one which is characterised by the most leading events either in the world of the dead or the world of the living, and all really big people are therefore to be found in this plane. We shall come to the details later on; for the present, the scope is limited to the general outline of the plane. What does Surya signify? In the oriental terminology, it is the all-pervading Sun; the English equivalent is not as forceful as the Indian word. Surya at once gives an idea of power, vitality, strength and brilliance. So much for the title. The population in this plane is very scanty and only runs into thousands and the reason is quite obvious. We have seen before that three factors decide the classification of the soul into middle or higher class. The qualification which is so essential in this loka is absent in a large majority of cases, and that is 'ambition'. At the same time, it holds good that the absence of the other three factors may turn the scale the other way. Only a spirit who has the other three factors in due proportions and, over and above that, has some strong ambition can aspire to be placed in the fifth plane.

We were talking of the nature of spirits in general who could dream of entering into the Surya Loka. This loka is not near other planes but is at a considerable distance and this shows the importance attached to this plane. The conditions of existence are not as calm as we experience in the Chandra Loka. On the contrary, we are in an atmosphere of bustle and activity which is so pleasing to spirits of my type, and perhaps, to my mediums too. In a way those, who feel like working, find themselves stationed in an admirable place. There is plenty of work to do and I can quote you cases where, due to scarcity of workers, people from the fourth plane were admitted among us.

Ambitious Spirits

We have already spoken of the qualifications which entitle a spirit to be in the fifth plane; but a careful analysis of the persons here gives us an idea of their ambitious nature. You will not find a single spirit here doing nothing. Everybody is found thinking and devising his or her own plane. Their ambitions are of two types—one regarding their own betterment in the spiritual world and then in the material existence down below. The second is their fervent desire to help other spirits even at the cost of their own interests. But one may be anxious to know whether any such ambitions have been realised. I can but give a rough idea about it, because I have never made any serious attempt to ascertain the exact number of cases in which such desires were realised. Yet, I am on sure grounds when I say that at least 40 per cent of good ambitions are realised. What constitutes ambitions? Bad or wicked desires are not regarded ambitions at all; only desires backed by good motives and sound canons of conduct are classed as ambitions. Of these too, those acts inspired by a spirit of public service are regarded as pure ambitions and in the long run, it pays the spirit who does cherish such aims. The investment is sound; yet it is not agreeable to many because there is no definite reward promised, and a detailed survey would indicate that pure ambitions are very rare.

Administrative Work

Every form of government requires persons to operate the system which is planned out by persons at the top. In the world of the living, we find that recruitment of officers is made by competitive examinations which are so designed as to test the general ability of the persons required. In a similar way, in the spirit world, too, Yama Raj has to make definite plans regarding the persons to be taken up for the administrative department. Naturally there is no competitive examination and some other device is employed, Yama Raj has made it a rule that those spirits who are not in the fifth plane are not to be allowed to take part in general administration; but he has made one exception and that proviso is for allowing the elementals to help in investigations. The divine regulation makes it clear that only spirits of the Surya-loka can participate in the work of administration. It may be mentioned here that even among the spirits of the fifth plane, there is a difference of degree, if not of kind, in their level of intelligence. When work is to be assigned to different spirits, naturally that factor is to be borne in mind. In some of the sittings, with my mediums, I have found them urging that every plane was a unit by itself and that there should be no chance of there being any degree of difference in the intelligence of the spirits of any one plane.

I have very often endeavoured to convince them that when a university confers a degree on several persons it does not assure the people that all of them have the same amount of intelligence, and that in the same way, the plane is meant for denoting a class rather than a measure itself. From this it must be evident to my readers that sprits from the same plane can and do hold different positions in our world. In this volume, it may appear superfluous to give a catalogue of different posts woth the names of persons holding them; yet if time and space permit, some idea may be given though I am very doubtful in view of the fact that I shall have to take permission from Yama Raj. It is equally foolish to keep my readers in suspense and therefore I can say that most of the posts are either regarding the work in the Court which is described elsewhere in this book and the other type is chiefly concerned with the control, supervision and management of different planes.

If I were to describe the various posts held by spirits from this plane, it would be rather complex to follow; but it can be safely said that in every plane, right from the top to the bottom, the fifth-stage spirits will be found occupying posts of considerable importance. We have already seen, every plane has a presiding deity; but it would be impossible even for that divine spirit to look after every matter in detail and it is very necessary that some assistants should be appointed for proper and efficient control. What functions are delegated to such spirits is a matter of internal management and personal equation is the deciding factor. Yet from what I have seen and experienced, I feel that certain divine spirits give full control regarding problems of daily occurrence and only reserve for themselves problems which are new in nature and are grave enough to receive personal attention and care, from such high souls themselves; while in certain cases I have noted that they do not want to delegate even ordinary power regarding the usual administrative work and they feel delighted in wasting a major portion of their time in dealing with such problems though I may venture to say that the importance of such routine problems is so little that they hardly deserve to be termed as problems. But, taking a general view, it appears that the deity is the chief minister while the others are his councillors.

Energiser

It would appear from the above description that spirits of the fifth plane have a colossal amount of energy and vitality. The reason is rather peculiar and hard to believe, I myself, when in the fourth plane, refused to believe it and I managed to see Yama on that point. He agreed with me that the spirits had no body and therefore nothing was necessary to keep them fit. But he proceeded further and revealed to me that in view of the demand made on these spirits of the Surya Loka, some help was deemed necessary and that took the shape of some condensed vapour containing a peculiar divine substance which I do candidly admit I have never seen nor drunk; but its presence in the atmosphere in the Surya Loka gives the spirits the necessary energy.

Presiding Deity

This loka being very active finds itself entangled in many problems of its own. They may be either relating to the spirits' personal affairs or certain things regarding administration, and very often a conflict between the spirits arises on a certain issue which has therefore got to be taken up by a very powerful authority and we find that 'god himself', popularly known as Shree Vishnu Bhagwan, tries to settle all important affairs, though most of the work is delegated to efficient assistants of His own. He is of course the best administrative Head in the whole of the administrative corps.

SIXTH PLANE — THE SWARGA LOKA

The Swarga Loka

The Surya Loka is so tempting that persons like me do not desire to go to the sixth one which is called the Swarga Loka. I need not state the reasons which lead me to this particular conclusion and therefore we proceed further. Swarga Loka is just near the Surya Loka and there is no great difference between the two planes. It is very natural that there are only a few thousand spirits in this plane and most of them have proved themselves worthy of being classed as sixth-stage spirits. The factors which decide the case are somewhat different from those of the Surya Loka. Ambition does not seem to play an important part and we find that most spirits of the sixth plane are not ambitious. On the contrary, calmness and such other attributes are of considerable use to them. But, it should not be for a moment deduced that intelligence is not required, because that quality is necessary in every stage in general and in this stage in particular. Calm people with little brains are no good for the sixth plane; yet this may not be invariably true nor do I claim any personal touch as I have never had the honour of visiting the Swarga Loka.*

Happy Souls

What does Swarga indicate? In Indian languages, it means the Heaven. The ideal to be hankered after is perfect happiness. It may be doubted whether spirits have any great perception of happiness as they have no physical existence. But the spirits identity has of course an idea of relative happiness or otherwise, though the concept of happiness is different here from that which is current in the world of the living of in other stages of spirit life. The spirit is happy at the idea of being promoted to this plane of eminence; he can look back with a certain amount of happiness, that his progress has been satisfactory so far; and he can look forward with a certain amount of confidence to salvation as a possible goal, which will release him from the care and trouble of births and deaths. Thus, one who is among the Swarga-loka-people considers this promotion as a stepping stone to further advancement leading up finally to the most coveted goal, Moksha or salvation.

---

* On the 10th May, 1937 we were informed that Sir Arthur Conan Doyle has been transferred to the Swarga Loka.

Cold Spirits

My flattering description of the spirits of the sixth plane might seem to be untrue to those who may have come into contact with spirits of the Surya Loka. The reason is not far to seek, because the usual complaint against them is their slow or dull response which appears to us so chilling, and we are sometimes led to believes that they are not the same persons or that they have lost their brain. But, have you not seen in your own world many instances in which your relative or your friend becomes cold and the popular reason assigned is that the person in point has become very rich or that he is in a much higher position than before? A person like me who would go behind such popular causes would find a rare logic behind it. When the sphere of activity of one person widely differs from that of the other one, a warm relationship becomes very difficult and the inevitable coldness results. In the same manner, when a spirit goes to the sixth plane, his activity changes and the material angle of vision becomes a divine one and if my analysis were to be applied, the sphere changes with the usual consequences.

Loss of Touch with the World

From the above picture of the life of the spirits of the Swarga Loka, it is evident that they have given complete satisfaction and obtained complete sympathy from the divine authorities and that all their desires are therefore satisfied to a large extent. In such a state of affairs, the materialistic ideal of life is conspicuous by its absence. When a high degree of contentment is reached, this is but natural. Many mediums are incompetent, either by their inferior brains or powers of attraction, to call such spirits; and broadly speaking, most of the Swarga Loka spirits are not within the reach of even fairly powerful mediums. This is a factor which goes a long way in reducing their possible touch with the world of the living. Over and above these points, we have already seen that the quality of ambition is also absent. In this way, a proper touch with the world is not feasible and, if I were to express some important spirit's views on this point, there is no need also for such high spirits to keep any strong connection with people beyond the World of the Dead. I however beg to differ, because, to my mind, it appears that it would be a case of gross selfishness on the part of those spirit's who have achieved a certain high status in their spiritual advancement. A really good person is he who even though he has no interest at stake keeps himself in touch with the world with philanthropic idea of assisting those who deserve some help.

Loss of Memory

It is difficult to give any definite reason for spirits in general, and spirits of the sixth plane in particular, losing their memory. But if my reasoning is correct, I think, that the fact of the contact with the other world being so nominal and insignificant comes in the way of their remembering events of their past life. In further elucidating the point, we might well remind ourselves of the absence of memory which results after a soul is given a new life. No person, when living, is able to give any idea of the life after death; the reason is obvious because there are no ways left open for him to continue his normal relations with the world which he has just left. In this way, we clearly see that even a nominal touch between the two worlds is very difficult to maintain and this is the cardinal point which is responsible for the gradual loss of memory. In the sixth plane, it is more so because there is the absence of strong desire to make such a contact possible. Furthermore, as Yama Raj would put it, there would be no end of 'troubles' and dissatisfaction if spirits were to remember every incident of their past life. I think, he is nearer the truth in this case.

Control is inevitable even in the Swarga. In popular parlance, the Swarga 'tends to' convey an idea of perfect harmony and we would never dream of control; but perfection is rare and even among finer people, there are certain problems which require a finer handling too. It is however fair to say that the number of disputes is much smaller than is the case in other lokas, because, after all, these are good people.

We have here a deity who is known as 'pavandev' in Indian mythology. He is the 'god' of Wind, as it were. Interpreted in scientific terms, he is in charge of the Transport Department. His methods of expediting cases are well known here and he therefore finds time to do other work over and above the work of control of the Swarga Loka.

SEVENTH PLANE — THE DEVA LOKA

The Deva Loka

The Deva Loka is the last plane in the world of the spirits. It is the highest rung in the ladder of progress. But it does not mean the end of life separate from the Creator. It is the best possible reward to get this promotion and I should think that only that man can aspire to be among such spirits who has lived, not one life but many lives which have proved to be of great use to humanity. But, all this applies only when we think of individual existence and not a combined existence with the Creator, because many will hold that this is not the highest reward possible and their idea of perfect happiness lies in merger which is known as Moksha. But I do not agree; but for the time being, I shall refrain from making any sweeping statements on that important issue. It is not fair on my part to term the persons of this loka as spirits, because even their identities are much higher than the souls of spirits of other stages, and we shall henceforth call them souls.

God-like Souls

Souls who have the good fortune to be placed in the Deva Loka, are usually selected after a great deal of anxious consideration on the part of the Court authorities, and a very limited number proves itself worthy of being promoted to this upper plane. What are the necessary qualifications is a natural question; but it being the sole concern of Yama Raj, it is not easy to give any clear cut idea of the standard by which spirits of the sixth plane are judged. But if I were to refer to case law, as it were though none really exists, it appears that the attribute of complete satisfaction is the proof round which the whole problem of promotion hangs. To make this quality perfect, calmness is also found helpful. If these two virtues are accompanied by the absence of fervent ambitions, they achieve a state of mind which is so essential for making a spirit different from the ordinary human being. They do not for a moment hanker after material achievements; they are cool and collected enough to think of higher problems of further spiritual advancement, either of their own or of their less fortunate fellow-beings. The only vice which is likely to corrupt their mental chastity is their snobbish mentality. Those persons therefore who are not intellectual snobs are given permanent but not eternal (because there is salvation) position in the plane called the Deva Loka. The Indian word brings out the correct picture of the mental condition and attitude in the souls in this particular plane. In our modern language, they may be termed god-like souls who are near our ideal of perfection. I am afraid, it is not in the power of the pen to give a realistic idea of these souls and I should say they are more than mere descendants of Adam.

No Touch with Mediums

It is a popular belief among mediums, both English and others, that by their powers of attraction no spirit dare resist their force. But, it will come as a bolt from the blue that every dead person comes only when he is inclined to talk with that particular medium. You must have seen cases where a sitting or a series of sittings are more or less failures and in cases of amateurs they would be forced to admit their inability to call a particular spirit. The reason is already given. It may be further added that spirits of all planes except those of the Deva Loka are nearly anxious to get an opportunity to talk with the people of the world which they have left. But, all of a sudden, a change occurs in the mind of the spirit when he is placed in the Deva Loka; and very often, he is anxious to avoid any sort of disturbance from the world beyond and this is the cause why mediums should not attempt to drag them in a world which for all practical purposes they have renounced; and to my mind it is a positive disservice to those divine persons who were among us some time before.

No Activity

Readers must be eager to know about the activities of such god-like souls. But, I am sure I will disappoint you when I say that in a deep atmosphere of calmness, no life of that sort exists. Does it not appear very strange to you ? I was really surprised to learn that such a high promotion means an end of one's active and industrious life. In my talk with the God of Death very recently, he explained to me that they are in the making for earning salvation. Naturally, it puts an end to the individual existence and this stage is designed to act as a prelude to the termination of such a type of life. Absence of activity is an evolutionrary process leading to the final goal.

Rest

Every soul who comes to the Deva Loka has received all sorts of necessary training during the course of many births which he had to take and this process of gradual change has made him what he is today. It is time for him to leave the world for ever and before he can do so, a period of rest is necessary, because the soul which is to be merged in the Great soul should be pure and free from all types of excitements. Just as we need rest after a strenuous year's work, in the same way when the great mission of life is over, a sigh of relief is a necessary prerequisite.

Control though inevitable in other stages of spiritual existence, is not regarded necessary here. Souls are free to act as they please and no rule of general conduct applies. But, if we go behind the language, every soul gets an interview with Vishnu or God by turns and during that meeting, any undesirable action is commented upon. In this way, a nominal indirect control is there; but it is better interpreted if we say that in this loka, there is the paternal guidance of the kind-hearted Vishnu.

CHAPTER V

THE THEORY OF REBIRTH

Hindu Belief — Buddhist Doctrine of Karma— Rebirths and Experience — Evolution—Reaping the Fruits of Past Life—Different types of Births—Number of Births Usually Required for Moksha — Missions of Life—Short Lives and their Missions—Concept of Spirit-identities—Change of Sex.

Hindu Belief

Many people do not admit the existence of spirits and the idea of reincarnation does not appeal to them. Moreover, no religion except the Hindu religion accepts such a concept. The Christians and Muslims believe in the theory of the Judgment Day and put their faith in the principle of Resurrection; but as we shall presently see such a state of stagnation is not to be found in the World of the Dead. On the other hand, the Hindu idea of rebirth is quite correct, for it does not presuppose a state of stagnation. Reasoning should convince us that such stagnation should have no place in the divine ordering of things, because our lives are after all meant for progress of some kind. Would it not be strange to believe and advocate that the spark of life, which leaves the body on death, does not enter some other body? The soul which departs from the body invariably does enter some other body, though such a change involves some lapse of time, because no authority however competent it may be, can fix a body before a soul can take charge of it. Furthermore, there is no scope for discussion in this case, when it is a matter of pure fact. I have endeavoured to examine the reason which justifies reincarnation, rather than prove the theory of rebirth, because such an attempt on my part would be futile, as it is a 'fait accompli'. The Hindus have known this fact for many many years and to them the idea would appeal no doubt; but to others it may sound quaint, though the present development in the spiritual and occult fields have led the people on that track.

Buddhist Doctrine of Karma

What purpose does rebirth serve in the general advancement of persons who are in the routine chain of births and deaths? This is the real crux of the problem of life. In the Hindu books, dealing with that subject, there is no direct analysis or the problem as a whole, and for some length of time the mystery of the mission of life was not made clear to the vast majority of the Indian people. Lest it may be misinterpreted, I wish to state that I have made no special study of religious books, and there are some spirits who hold that the Hindu religion by indirect or direct implications has given to the world the idea of Karma. I have no authority to flout that opinion; but, I am on surer grounds when I say that the Buddha, who flourished in India in the sixth century before Christ, made out for the first time a strong case in favour of the Karma theory, if at all it existed before. The whole exposition of the doctrine is so lucid, interesting and instructive, that I advise my readers to get an idea of that original contribution to the theory or Reincarnation and the real purpose of life. What is meant by Karma? The English translation would lead us to the word "deed". But only a shade of the real meaning of the original is expressed by that word. Karma at once makes one think of the consequences and after-effects of a particular action performed by a person. The theory goes on to express the idea in minute details, but the gist of the whole point is that the life of a person after death in the spirit-world is not of very great importance; but that particular person's soul, when given another birth, has to reap the fruits of the seeds which he has sown in his previous life. For his good actions, he gets adequate and ample rewards in the shape of material happiness and prosperity; while, for his bad deeds, he has to suffer, such sufferings taking the shape of setbacks which we come across in everyday life.

It is rather strange that no set-off is allowed and every action is to be repaid in kind though it means a bitter experience indeed. But, even a high person like the Buddha has apparently neglected the principle of Karma, because his teachings have never endeavoured to explain the influences which the same doctrine exercises in the spirit-world, and he has failed to perceive the concept of spirit identity. In the spirit-world also, good and bad actions have their effects on the spirit's life. But there is a vast difference, every action is not to be paid in kind. Yama Raj while deciding a particular case takes into account the good and bad deeds and he finds out the resultant effect and this effect in its turn decides the assignment of a plane. In this way we clearly see that the doctrine of Karma finds direct application both in the living and the dead worlds, with this difference that the principle of set-off applies to the spirit-world but 'not' to the living world.

Rebirths and Experience

The first thing which should strike a person interested in the Theory of Rebirth is the significance of births and deaths. What is the idea underlying this rotation of births and deaths? It is not difficult to understand it, if we believe in the evolution of the soul, regarding that vital part as a thing capable of further advancement and improvement and not as perfect and complete. If this assumption be true, the problem of educating a soul naturally confronts the Creator and he has evolved a system of progressively educating souls through the agency of the living world. If for a moment we assume that the soul were given a permanent body and death were abolished, the soul in its particular station of life would not after a certain stage be able to improve further and a limit would be reached which would spell nothing short of stagnation. We must therefore reject this assumption as absurd. As the only way of avoiding such a contingency, God has assigned limits to each birth and the period intervening between two births is Death and the life thereafter. These various births give souls the necessary experience without allowing them to reach a state of existence which can be called stagnation. It has been common knowledge that a soul sometimes gets a long life and sometimes a short one. The reasons which determine the span of life in one birth depend on the facts of each individual case; but it may be safely asserted that when a particular type of birth has done its work in the shape of giving the necessary education to the soul, the limit is reached. This limit may be short or long, just enough to allow a soul to reap the fruits of his past life. These details however do not concern us here; for the basic idea after all is to give experience and education to the soul.

Evolution

The general theory of Rebirth is placed before my readers attempting to show the idea and principles underlying the whole problem. We shall now examine how the process of evolution works out in practice. Evolution unlike revolution does not attempt to set the house in order in one birth, but by a long and gradual process, which is smooth enough in normal cases. It is the design of the spirit-world authorities to do that difficult task in a series of births, which is a long process indeed, but no human or divine brain so far has evolved any better system. How is the whole evolution programme planned out is an interesting point no doubt. When a soul is to be given a birth, he is not given a bad position in life, because the authorities send out souls, not with a view to test them, but to know their real worth. It is a mistake to assume that new souls start from the lowest point. Very often it is the reverse and new souls are placed in very good circumstances and surroundings to prove their worth. It is only when they either live a life not desirable in that birth or misuse certain opportunities, that they have to undergo rigid tests or prove themselves worthy of living a good life among a host of temptations and complications. But taking a good case, in which the soul has showed its worth, a better birth, with easier conditions of life and better opportunities to come out successfully, lies in store for him. We thus clearly see the motive behind the process of evolution. All that the Creator desires is the general advancement of all the souls. We may further say that the whole process is so well arranged that a soul gets all types of experiences and the varieties of birth provided are so many that there is no reason to doubt the usefulness of this method by which good results can be achieved. But some may feel doubtful of the whole exposition given by me because they know that the number of persons getting salvation is very small. I agree with them, but what I contend is that if all the opportunities given during various births are utilised properly, the final goal is not far off. But, in most cases, such happy exploitation of good occasions is not attempted or it is beyond ordinary human power and to this extent the ultimate goal becomes more and more remote.

Reaping the Fruits of Past Life

In the preceding paragraph, we have assigned too much importance to the process of evolution. But that is not the only idea underlying the whole scheme. One birth imparts certain legacies either good or bad, and the next birth visualises their actual realisation, and in its turn creates further obligations. In this fashion, the world goes on, till the soul is considered fit enough to be merged and no longer be in this world of the living, or of the dead. Thus, if the whole idea were to be expressed in brief, everybody incurs certain obligations and is required to make them good or exact, as the case may be, in the succeeding incarnations. This is reaping the fruits of the past life, the bad and good acts of that life having their own effects. I for one believe that in the world of the living too, a set-off should be allowed and only the balance, good or bad, should effect the person concerned. But since government does not usually listen and payment in kind continues so far, the only thing I can do is to suggest to the people concerned to organise and resort to collective action, because such matters receive adequate attention and care only when the authorities get an idea of the number of persons in favour of it. I know, however, or a person well versed in spiritual matters, who holds that such a step would make the world such that the idea of advancement would be completely defeated. The world would be too simple to afford any scope for high ideals of life or noble ideas of duty and sacrifice. The test would be diluted to a considerable degree and would lead us to believe that a stage of stagnation would be reached. My idea differs widely and I would like to know from such people why they believe that the world would be too simple to live in. In a way, I believe, the simpler the material world, the better the type of education afforded. We see however that in the present circumstances, the Creator seems to make the lives of souls as complex as possible and most of us are forced to undergo very rigid test. My idea of a pleasant simple world is not considered worthwhile putting into practice. There is one satisfaction though in the fact that everybody reaps what he has sown and if one attempts to lead as simple a life as possible, the further legacies would be reduced to a large extent and the purpose in view can be achieved only to a small extent.

Different Types of Births

Everyone of us has to take a certain number of births. But all these births do not form so many classes. On the other hand, the types of births are few in number though the stations of life may vary to a considerable extent.

Among the chief types of births, there is one category known as 'comfortable birth', which is regarded as quite good because it makes it possible to be quite successful in the material world. Hardships are few and far between, there are ample opportunities for doing good to oneself and to others. Furthermore, the duration of life in this type of birth is fairly long, and in every respect, fair play is offered.

The second type is 'luxurious birth', which means the best station in life. The surroundings are so favourable that a person who is wise enough is bound to make good progress during his life in the world and even after such an existence is extinct. If I were to put it correctly, hardships or setbacks in life do not exist and there lies before you a path strewn with roses; and there can be therefore unchecked advancement. Furthermore, it is evident that God gives such a type of birth to those who are likely to progress and are still new. But, the grave danger which stares, as it were, in the face of these seemingly happy souls is temptation or 'maya'. It is easy to say that such hurdles should not prove an impediment to spiritual progress. But it is easier said than done, because, the fascination for such worldly joys and pleasures is very often so strong that restraint is out of question. If by accident or design such control can be exercised, the future of the soul concerned is bright; but if he falls a victim to this glorious 'maya', such a birth may never come again.

The third type is the 'birth full of troubles, toil and poverty'. Here perhaps the 'maya' does not exist; but its glamour is none the less as acute as before. In such a birth or in such a wretched existence, no ideals can be expected nor is the soul expected to do any good to others. If he manages to live a useful existence and not be a burden to others and if he is able to make both ends meet by fair means, he will be deemed to have done all that could be expected of him. But the painful existence and awful surroundings tend to drive the person to lose all his reason and this may force him to use underhand means to get some relief. This sort of birth is in a way the acid test which can be applied to souls of all types. There are a few other classes or sub-classes of births, but I think, these three should serve to illustrate the purposes for which the births are employed in helping the souls to come out. Naturally my readers would like me to give some interesting details; but unfortunately there are some restrictions which prevent me from supplying them here. I would be the last person to shield my inabilities under the plea of restrictions; but here it is a fact.

Number of Births Usually Required for Moksha

We have been talking of births all through, but I think it is now desirable to give an idea of the number of births usually required for achieving the final goal, 'the merger'. Among the Hindus, or the Indians in general, there is a belief current that 84 lakhs of births have to be taken before one can think of salvation; but I am not so sure of this because there is no such stipulated limit and every case depends on its merits. There may be cases where even 84 lakhs of births may not earn the coveted 'moksha'. At the same time instances of persons getting salvation in say a few hundred births are not very rare. The number largely depends on the quality of the soul. But, if we were to confine ourselves to the middle class or the vast majority of souls, they nearly take about 80 to 90 thousand births before they can think of the divine merger. It may be that instead of 84 lakhs, it was 84 thousand in the original books. But due to public memory being notoriously short, such an exaggeration may have crept in. It is diffcult to give any clear cut number and I do not want to make a sweeping remark over such a delicate point. But in normal cases, my estimate is very nearly correct. Furthermore, even the authorities cannot know the required number because that depends upon the deeds of the soul in previous births. There is no royal road to attain salvation. It is necessary for a soul to pass through various kinds of ordeals and vicissitudes in the shape of births which are certainly not comfortable. I often feel that most persons have such a psychological way of viewing things that they refuse to grasp the fundamentals of leading a good and useful life. They can visualise things only when presented in a concrete form. Thus, experience has to be gathered and not learnt; and this accounts for the slow and tardy development of most of us, in spite of the fact that we do not make our debut on the lowest rung of the ladder of progress. If our Creator had not been so kind and if we had to begin from the bottom of the deep spiritual ocean, even the famed Hindu mythical 84 millions of births would have failed to achieve the desired goal. It is a pity that God does not become kind enough to allow a soul, who has been stumbling over the rock of advancement repeatedly to progress and to earn promotion to a higher stage. Once the soul is created and let loose under favourable circumstances, he has to show his own worth and to earn 'moksha'.

Missions of Life

I shall now turn my attention to a most complex and delicate subject. The importance of the problem of the mission of life makes it necessary for me to make at least a passing reference to the subject. At this moment, I confess my weakness and that is that I have, or my brain has, failed to single out even a few outstanding missions of life, much less a single one. But one cannot blame me for this inability, because I have made a constant endeavour to find the way out of the wood. In my discussion with the God of Death, I have learnt, learnt with some satisfaction that people who are superior to me in most respects have met with nearly the same result. What is then the cause? I ask my readers. If my ability does not fail to analyse the problem under normal circumstances, is it not the multiplicity of births as well as of souls that is responsible for diverse missions of life in existence? Whatever may be the explanation assigned to the fact of there being diverse missions of life, it is certain that such diversity does exist. Why such a number of missions should be in existence is a question which would give good food for reflection and speculation to an intelligent man. But I think it is none of our business to go into these details.

I now propose to take up some outstanding missions and give an analytical account of them. The first and the most important (so far as it relates to the popular notions) mission of life is 'self-betterment and gratification of personal desires'. The words are in a way self explanatory. People, with very narrow ideas of existence, are tempted to hold this as their ultimate goal. They in most cases have never cared, or have not the power, to think in a rational manner. Such a class or people is characteristically composed of spirtis of the third stage or the Tapa Loka. They are middle class people with ideas which certainly do not do credit to the conception of a good and well lived human life. This may be an exaggeration, yet it is more or less correct insofar as it attempts to depict the class. The concept of self-betterment is or can be interpreted in one's own way. But keeping in mind broad divisions, it means good of one's self and family. Even this is not clear as the word 'family' has in course of time assumed different meanings; but our typical man does not go beyond the very narrow circle of his family. This much for the quantitative aspect of betterment. But we have neglected the qualitative aspect so far. The betterment in this respect can assume two forms; one material and the other, spiritual. Gratification of worldly desires including passions and baser instincts of our race form the former sort of betterment. Such people can never progress as their actions would be of such a nature that every act would involve the 'I'. They would never think of others and would not even shudder when injuring the interests of others. I for one would say that such people deserve no place on our earth. But, that apart, the divine authorities also treat them with contempt. The idea of spiritual betterment has found favour among the Hindus. Renouncing the world for self-betterment is a common thing in India. Here the aim is not deprecated as the person tries to attain the goal which is divine. But the only thing which is bad is that the person does not shoulder the troubles and risks which are meant for him, and in this way he makes his period of training short indeed with the usual consequences. Furthermore, even during the period of training, he stays away from the world for all practical purposes, and in this way that particular incarnation is said to have failed in its basic motive, and I for one would call it no training. Anyway, it is not a good and noble way of leading life, which presents very few opportunities for testing and training. But, I have found that such people do progress and that too fairly rapidly.

Now coming to the second mission of life, we come to a class of people who do not care to think of tomorrow and their mission is one, which can be aptly described as 'aimless existence'. They are very peculiar in this respect and resemble animals more than men, and in my opinion they are absolutely unfit for birth as human beings. The only thing that makes them work is the problem of keeping the body and soul together. If they can manage to get their bread without any trouble, they would not exert themselves. In this way they lead a very low life even though their character may be good. The ideals of high social service or status are conspicuous by their absence. They never aspire to progress either materially or spiritually. Perhaps they seem to advocate stagnation and they are certainly stagnation incarnate. I personally hate these people, but in our world there is no word of contempt for them. At the most, they are reminded of the useless life they have led in the trial-judgment; but in no case an appeal is made to bring about a change in their outlook. It is evident, of course, that they have fewer opportunities offered in the next birth and this acts as a further hindrance to their progress. I wonder how many births would be enough to kindle that urge which would lead to progress. It is a moot point but I would say it is a difficult task to induce any change in their attitude. At least, that has been my experience.

Thirdly, we have the very noble and perhaps the best mission and that is the 'mission of service'. I, for one, feel that if at all our life is to remain distinct from and superior to other lives and if we are to make our incarnation successful, the whole of our life should be dominated or controlled by that high quality which begins from duty and widens itself into service and that is why it has been compared to a spiral spring. Duty is a thing which is not a virtue; but this may sound paradoxical, because in every thing that is said about duty, it is referred to as perhaps the highest virtue. But I hold that duty to oneself is an inevitable thing and if we, with all our human intelligence, do perform this duty, there is nothing abnormal. As a matter of fact, we are performing the most natural act which God has ordained us to do. Now supposing for a moment one of us fails to perform the duty to oneself, it is a vice no doubt. Thus, non-performance is a crime, but faithful adherence is not a virtue. In this way, it must have been clear to you that everyone of us should do his duty towards himself because if such acts were not done, the progress of the world both spiritual and material would be checked. This leads me to express a view that performance of duty cannot be classed as a mission, though there are some who do maintain that it does form a mission. I leave this fact to be judged by my readers. There exists a fine line of difference between duty and service. Whereas duty relates to oneself, service relates to all except one's own self. Furthermore, there can be only one type of duty while service can be subdivided into two major classes. One is service without any desire for reward or even a partial return; the other kind of service is rendered with a definite idea of a complete or partial return in some form. Turning our thoughts to this latter type of service, it is evident that it falls short of the noble and lofty ideal which is attached to this sacred word. If it is rendered with an idea of getting the full reward, in my opinion, it ceases to be service; but if partial reward is expected, it is certainly an act which pleases divine authorities and to that extent the person concerned is said to prove that he has lived a useful life. Some may argue that even a desire for spiritual advancement, which may act as an inducement, should take that deed away from the category of service This is logically true; but as there are rules in the courts of the world of the living, which make certain things legal by its approval, in the same fashion, our court has regarded this particular desire as absolutely valid and there is no scope for further discussion.

Now coming to the mission of 'pure service', I for one am

inclined to think and that too with good reasons that such an ideal cannot exist and will not exist in the imperfect human world and if I may venture to say it is not even found in the spirit world. Perhaps, you may feel that I am dogmatic in my views; but before you form that idea, do think about the abstruse principle of service in the widest sense. Everyone of us from the very birth, as it were, does every act with the idea of receiving some good out of it, and this particular instinct does not disappear even with the passage of time. Human nature itself is against pure service. Perhaps this instinct makes us materialistic and we form a distinct class by ourselves. It is rather difficult to pass any judgment about the mental trend of the divine beings; but I am sure that there are certain moments when they also forget the concept of pure service and become a prey to the material instinct. I have not enough courage to give further details on this point. Coming to the world of the living, there are people who do certain acts without any idea of gaining anything from them. But such acts are far and few between, since it often happens that though the service is rendered without at the moment any desire for reward, after it is performed the human mind feels that there should be some reward from the party who received the benefit. In this way, the lurking desire creeps in and shatters the very roots of pure service to pieces. I would quote my own example. When I thought of writing this book in Mahabaleshwar in the year 1936, I had an idea of pure service. Subsequently, as the book developed on original lines, and when I received some information that it is well spoken of, a lurking desire crept in my mind that I should get a good reward for my labours either in the shape of a better stage or an excellent birth. I did not deliberately think in this way; but very gradually such ideas crystallised in my mind. This is an adequate explanation for illustration this natural weakness of the human mind. Thus, it seems to me that the idea of pure service is rather abstruse and difficult for our society to adopt. But, at the same time, I do not hold that we should not attempt are sure to prove futile; but you may rest assured that everyone of us gets a few rare opportunities when it is possible to put theory into practice.

I do not want to go into further details about other missions of life because they fall into one of the three classes I have described, with some changes, and in some cases there is a mixture of one or two to them. Our society is essentially dynamic and clear cut divisions do not exist.

Turning our eyes to the results we get by having some definite mission of life, I feel the position is clear enough, because the nobler the mission of life the better are the deeds performed, and when those deeds have some good points about them the cumulative effect is spiritual and material advancement.

Short Lives and their Missions

We can understand all missions of life, but we are confronted with some difficulty when we find cases where the life is too short, sometimes even less than one year. Can such souls have anything to do in the world to which they are sent? Yama Raj explains such cases by saying that babies die, not to get experience themselves, but they are simply instruments to give experience to their parents. Or it may be that for the bad conduct of a particular soul, the rigors of death are the only punishment and a short life is given in such cases to furnish an occasion for inflicting that punishment. This explains the phenomenon of still-births also. Short lives of say four or five years or even more may be needed in some cases to complete a period of time, and not to add any experience, for granting promotion from one stage to the higher one. These explanations may be true; but do they not seem to be based on considerations devoid of human feelings?

Concept of Spirit-identities

So far we have talked about the spiritual world; but the soul has to go back to the material world. This brings our an interesting problem and that is: During the material life, does the soul sever his connection with the world of the dead? If we were to think as living people do, the soul, as soon as he is born, has to leave the spirit world completely. But this is not true. Early Hindus thought and perhaps the modern Indians also think in the same strain, though I feel this was due to the fact that regular spiritual talks were not conducted. But the facts are that a soul though indivisible has two bodies or forms as it were. The chief form is the soul which goes to the material world, for training, and for all practical purposes this is the soul in the popular sense. But, the other form, which in its powers is roughly one eighths of the main form, is the soul so far as the spirit-world is concerned. But, it is not called a soul but a spirit. Such a spirit is, as it were, kept to give a correct idea of the soul concerned. This spirit in the language of the Court is called an identity of so and so. Identity is a word which just expresses the meaning, and it is, as it were, a faithful reproduction of the soul. Perhaps this idea of the identity may appear strange; but when you, spiritualists, find that some people even though they are reborn can still talk, it is beyond doubt that there is some agency, which does the work of talking, and this particular phenomenon can only be explained by the concept of spirit-identities. The proof for the existence of such identities can be easily found in practical sittings.

Change of Sex

Before concluding the chapter, about the theory of rebirth, it is desirable to discuss the problem of the change of sex. Those who have no belief in reincarnation have abstained from discussing the point. I do not know whether the Hindus have bothered about it. I am not sure and therefore this statement is open to correction. But whatever the world may think about it, God wants to give various types of births and therefore. He gives both types of births. Thus, a person may be a male in one birth and a female in the next one. But very often it happens that there are series of births during which time the soul does not change the sex. But, it is certain that the proportion does not go beyond the limit of 30-70, that is, a soul has to take at least 30 per cent of the total births as a male and 70 per cent as a female or vice versa. But in normal cases, the proportion is nearly 50-50. The change of sex is a normal thing, though I am sure this statement will come as a surprise to most of you.

CHAPTER VI

A DAY IN THE LIFE OF A SPIRIT

Environment — No Support Necessary — No Particular Duty — No Physical Senses — No Need for Food or Shelter — Attendance at Trials — Assignment of Special Duties — Attendance on Gods — Petty Investigations — Visit to the World — Peep into the Future — Daily Routine.

Environment

So far we have been describing various phases of the unknown world, but it is high time that you should be more intimately informed about the daily life of spirits. But before we begin our tale of their daily life, it is desirable that some illusions about our spirit-world should be removed. This world does not differ to an appreciable extent from the world of the living insofar as the natural atmosphere is concerned. In all the places there is the normal atmosphere though it is certainly rarified and useless for human consumption. But, as most of you must be knowing, spirits do not have to take the trouble of breathing, as they have no lungs. All physical senses are conspicuous by their absence and it is taken for granted in this book that readers by a little stretch of imagination are able to visualise such a being. Winds also find a place in the world of the dead. But fortunately, or unfortunately, there is no rainfall. In normal cases, these elements are calm, and do not in any way prove to be a hindrance to spirits.

Furthermore, we have also the inevitable phenomena of days and nights. Of course, we have no seasons because variations in the temperature have no effect on us. In this way it must be clear that normal natural conditions exist; but there is one great difference between the two worlds; in the living world, these elements play a very important part in the lives of people, while in the spirit-world, they have no effect.

No Support Necessary

Apart from this difference just pointed out, there is also a great difference in the two worlds ; in this that in the world of the humans, there is the earth is to support the material beings. It is very difficult to imagine a world without the earth, because human beings who have physical senses require some support to carry on their normal work to gratify their desires. I am sure that human existence without such a concrete form would be impossible and if the earth were to disappear, human existence would come to an end. Among the Hindus, there is a belief that when there are many people away from the path of virtue and the Creator feels that it is better to wind up his Creation, He would destroy the earth. But I differ from this ill-founded view, because divine beings rarely advocate such a destructive policy. In a way this digression has no place here. Resuming our main theme, we find that the spirit-world is a world without the earth. These identities having no physical senses do not require the concrete support which human beings need badly. It is, I know, very difficult to imagine correctly the world of spirits because the human conception of a world is always associated with an idea of some concrete existence. I also think that the power of the pen would fail to give correct touches to the rough picture I have tried to portray before my readers. But if you can somehow conceive of a being devoid of all senses except the mental faculties, such a world would not appear inconceivable to you, though I will not blame those minds who refuse to grasp it. A spirit is not a being with a body or a form. It is, at its best, a reservoir of energy or a spark of life or the guiding force of human beings. As electricity is an energy which cannot be caught, the spirit in the same manner cannot come under human sway of influence.

No Particular Duty

Spirits are better described as identities because the word spirit conveys a wrong meaning insofar as it tends to give an idea of separate existence. Spirit-life in a way there is none; and we spirits are merely shadows of the real beings who are in the mortal world, and, it is very natural that, these shadows should have no particular life of their own, though they do in a way represent the soul's past life. It is however erroneous to hold that no life for identities exists at all. The distance between the soul on the Earth and the spirit here justifies a separate life, though, as you will subsequently notice, the life which they lead is hardly worth the name.

The beings who form the spirit-world are not in a position to undertake any regular work. All the senses except that of the mind are taken away from the spirits, and this reason is enough to justify their inability or failure to take up any work, which would require constant effort. Some argue that if their mental faculty is strong, they should be in a position to take up duties that relate to such mental faculty, and verily spirits with adequate brain power do make use of their energy. The Court authorities have therefore always abstained from assigning any duties to all spirits; only those who show exceptional willingness and ability are requested to assist the government.

No Physical Senses

As we have seen before, in this chapter, and perhaps elsewhere too, the spirit is bereft of all physical senses, and it would be very difficult for you to visualise such a being. If among living persons one of them were to lose, say, his eyes, or ears, his existence would be simply horrible. From such sufferings of humanity, you can perhaps form an idea of the pitiful life of the spirit. But then how does he carry on? Perhaps, it is difficult to explain. It will not enter your brains that we talk quite freely without any power of speech. We catch your call all right without any hearing faculty. How can this be explained? The only explanation I can place before you is the fact that God knows that we have no senses and therefore permits His divine powers to come to our aid. So much for receiving and giving ideas and information among ourselves. But with the living people our position is very weak. We have to make strong efforts to convey our ideas; and we are not able to give proofs to them of our existence.

No Need for Food or Shelter

A spirit, if you can see in the right perspective, is in a position to live without food. Having no physical existence, he does not require any food and if he were supplied with any, he has no powers to eat. The spark of energy he represents does not require any help in the shape of some food to carry on. But it appears to me that some help is necessary and perhaps, the divine authorities see their way in this respect. How they do it, or whether they do it or not is a complete mystery to me. But it is a fact that the identities are always quite fit. The problem of food is connected with that of shelter. The conditions in this connection are the same as in the case of food; shelter is not needed; and as a matter of fact, nothing is provided. But it is true that when we go out for a stroll, we do like places with good climatic conditions, though the reason for such preference is mainly a psychological one. This view is mine; but some hold that spirits are affected by climatic changes. When however I requested a person, holding such a view to explain and substantiate it, he was not in a position to do so and I continue to hold to my belief of the reason being a psychological one only.

Attendance at Trials

In the preceding pages, we have dealt with the Court more or less completely and given some information about the attendance of spirits. Now we shall go into some further details. Trials are conducted for judging the souls who return after completing their term of life. The deeds of the past life are placed before the Court and an analytical survey of the past existence is carried out. Thus, the Court authorities have deemed it desirable that these decisions and discussions should be utilised for some good purpose. What purpose they can serve is clear enough. It is certainly the best possible training ground for spirits. If spirits were to attend the Court trials and take a live interest in various proceedings, described in a previous chapter, these are bound to help them in advancing both spiritually and materially. These trials are conducted so carefully and efficiently that a spirit is sure to find something definitely interesting and useful for him. Perhaps my earlier description may have led you to believe that the judgments are merely sermons or threats from Yama. But it is far from that. That Court authorities have however never made attendance at trials compulsory. If I were consulted on this point, I should certainly say that every spirit should devote some time of the day in hearing trials, because there is no other institution or place where a spirit may get some guidance or help regarding his betterment. But if he were to devote, say, an hour or two at the Court, the amount of knowledge which he would secure would be substantial and it may stand him in good stead in his next life. Here I may make it clear that very advanced spirits are not likely to receive any benefit by attending the Court; but they can certainly help in the administration.

Assignment of Special Duties

From the above description we might perhaps conclude that spirits have no work to do; but that is not universally true. From the chapter on the Seven Stages of souls, it is apparent that only spirits of the fifth plane or the Surya Loka are in a position to do some work. I have already explained to you before that other spirits are not able to help in general administration. But if you remember elementals have also considerable powers in this respect. The Court has therefore, made use of these two classes of spirits for carrying on its work. This is not however the normal duty of the spirits; it is a special duty, assigned to them. Thus, some spirits are made use of in investigations, while others are useful in recording events of importance, and others yet are used for pleading cases and so on. As I have discussed previously, the whole edifice of court administration rests on the honorary services rendered by spirits of the Surya Loka. I have no idea of belittling the share of the elementals; but their work is not honorary, because they can only be persuaded to work if some definite reward is forthcoming for them. Whether honorary or paid, however, they help the Court in many ways. The powers, which they possess, melt away the most formidable obstacles in the work of difficult investigations. Their methods may not be perfect; but the results which they achieve are simply marvellous, and the Court is more concerned with the results than with the technique. In this way, we see that 'special duties' are assigned; but no spirit is forced to take up any work against his will. But as a matter of fact so many spirits are anxious to work that there is not enough work for all of them and the problem of forcing spirits to do work against their will does not arise. Some further duties are given to spirits, willing to work in their own planes or stages; and these duties are called 'domestic duties' or 'local duties'. They chiefly relate to the problems of spirits 'inter se' and are of smaller importance. Spirits of every stage are allowed to do such work, though preference is given to Surya Loka spirits. In this way, we have clearly laid before us the whole problem of special duties which are generally asigned to spirits in general and spirits of the Surya Loka in particular. It may sound peculiar that the main burden of administration is shouldered by the Surya Loka people; but when we analyse their powers and will-force, we come to the conclusion that the authorities are justified in putting their confidence in them. One might perhaps argue that if such a monopolistic position is enjoyed by them, other spirits would not get chances to show their worth. But if they have failed to come up to the fifth-plane level, there is no reason why they should grumble about the absence of opportunities offered to them.

Attendance on Gods

So far, we have been describing duties which relate to general administration. There are other duties however which do not come under this classification; but it would be out of place to discuss all such duties. We shall, therefore, take up only a few of them. One of the most important of such duties is attendance on gods. Perhaps at this juncture, it might be expedient to define a 'god', or a divine soul. The point as a matter of fact will come for discussion towards the end of this book. But it will serve our purpose for the time being to define them as souls who have been able to conquer the weaker side of human nature and to that extent are free from worldly desires. Self-control and service dominate their lives and we call them gods. Such beings who have proved themselves worthy of guiding other spirits' destinies are naturally overburdened with work, and do require some other spirits to help them in carrying out the duties entrusted to them. It is desirable to eliminate the illusion about attendance on gods, because in Indian mythology, the picture is penned in such a way that we are led to believe that gods require the attendance of spirits to look after their personal comforts. This is erroneous because gods never require spirits to look after them. On the contrary they always advocate the true spirit of service. It is only in their official capacity that they seek other spirits' help. Even for this work, nobody is forced to help them, and the service is absolutely voluntary. Very often it is difficult to select workers because there are many spirits who offer their services; and here also the fifth plane soul gets preferential treatment.

Petty Investigations

In the preceding paragraph, we said that gods require some help and it is very common that such aid is necessary in solving problems which confront every plane. This duty thus in a way falls under the classification of domestic or local duties. It should not be supposed that petty investigations are not carried on by the Court; we find as a matter of fact that a large number of spirits are used by the court for this purpose. The work does not call for high intellectual powers and any willing worker is allowed to do it. After the inquiry is over, the spirit concerned is asked to give a complete report of it and it is here that we find that some spirits fail to carry out the work entrusted to them. But the consequences are not serious, because this work does not deal with important problems. In a way it trains up spirits to perform responsible duties.

Visit to the World

So far as the life of spirits is concerned, there is no reason why they should go to the world of the living. Nature does not desire that there should be any active and close touch between the living and the dead. But this should in no way convey the wrong and sometimes popular idea that God is against such communications. The only thing that the Court authorities maintain is that there being no need of maintaining such a touch, they need not facilitate such meetings. At the same time, they express their willingness if such meetings could be conveniently arranged, and that too without disturbing the spirits from the duties assigned to them. Thus, if we were to analyse these words, or rather read between the lines, it is clear that they do not give any active support to either mediums or spirits. Even the reward which mediums get for doing this work is very little. But taking things as they are, it seems to me that it is the duty of those who have the power to invoke spirits to devote some time from their leisure moments for mutual advantage. But some might doubt my words, because they might be holding that no mutual advantage ensures from such spiritual meetings. I do not want to challenge their doubts, but I would request them to imbibe the ideal of service either to the dead or the living. Looking at the more practical side of the question, we find that there are enough spirits and mediums to hold frequent and successful sittings and the part played by the professional class is also considerable. Some of the intelligent spirits make it a point to use a certain part of their spare time in going to various mediums. If we were to take my case, I devote roughly 4 to 5 hours per day among my mediums. The same is the case with spirits who take a very active part in the life of the spirits. But, is difficult to measure the gain obtained by such spirits, because no concrete profit can ever be obtained through these meetings. If these meetings were a normal phenomena, people would not have mixed up the idea of profit; but as it is, we give an abnormal colour to a simple event. We must therefore make it absolutely clear that such a meeting is just an ordinary meeting and cannot possibly admit of any idea of gain. Gradually, people are realising that spirits are not superior to human beings; on the contrary, they are deprived of certain powers which the living persons possess. Further, we find that roughly 70 per cent of the spirits are called by mediums or they have managed to talk with a medium some time in their lives. We will rarely find a spirit who has not been called by a medium. Why is this? This reason is clear enough. Every spirit after departing from the world of the living, has a lurking desire to be in touch with a living person and preferably with a relative or a friend, and this instinct is always strong among most spirits. This is why nearly all spirits are eager to catch the first opportunity which they come across to establish communication with the living. It is also true that there are some spirits who hate going to mediums; they by their very nature, are reserved and never feel like talking for a long time. The number of such spirits is however very small. Further more, we find that there are certain mediums who persist in maintaining touch with one particular spirit only; but that is not very desirable, for after some time they know each other so well that it does not prove very useful to either of the parties. It is in the interest of all to call various spirits; and spirits should also make it a point to have as many medium friends as possible. In this way the two worlds will tend to become one unit and there will be no large gaps between the two types of persons of the same Creator. In a way this book is designed to fill in an important gap in the systematic literature relating to the life in the other world. Spirit-communications are not yet perfect and that is the cause why many people doubt the very existence of spirits and why those too who agree to talk with them get disappointed when they are not able to get details of the spirits' past life, little realising the short-comings of the spirits. It is certain that the mechanism is not foolproof and to a small degree impersonation is practised. But it is also true that such occurrences are not many insofar as the number of such spirits is not large. Fun can only exist for a short time and therefore long drawn sittings are very probably genuine. To sum up, such meetings between mediums and spirits are very practicable and both the worlds should co-operate in devising a perfect method of making such talks as successful as possible.

Peep into the Future

It is a popular belief that spirits or dead persons' souls are superior to human beings and attain divine powers. People seem to assume that as soon as the soul goes to the other world, it gains an insight into the past, present and future and thus becomes a person who can foresee all future events at a moment's notice. But, when we come to concrete facts, we must realise that the soul does not get this insight and he remains where he was; even his mental powers do not increase. On the contrary, I am afraid, he loses some of his mental abilities and his memory is definitely shorter than before. Some of you might be startled to realise the really limited extent of the powers of spirits: but when once you come to realise this, you will agree with me that spirits are not in a position to predict future events. The belief that they are in better position to guess the future is more or less correct. They, being in an unbiased state of mind, can look forward without fear or favour and to that extent their guesses may be correct. But, this is possible only when the full data are laid open before a spirit who is willing to think over the material so presented to him. Ill-planned data or concealed facts are a severe handicap to the spirit concerned. Further, if a particular spirit is consulted very often, he gradually develops a bias towards that party and ultimately his guesses become mixed products of judgment and favour or prejudice. Assuming for a moment, that the guess is unbiased, even then the probability of their turning out correct is hardly 50 per cent. This particular work is not the normal function of the spirits and that is the reason why we should not blame them for their guesses being incorrect. At the same time, there is no objection if such guesses are taken in a lighter mood and treated as semi-jokes.

Daily Routine

Every life is wedded to a routine and in a way a routine is an inseparable accident which the human and the spirit lives have to experience. Human life is known to us and I need not describe its routine; but we shall now take up the spiritual life, as it is from day to day. Spirits like human beings also need some rest and they utilise night for that purpose. Rest is not to be confounded with sleep because spirits having no bodily existence are not in a position to sleep. Their mind gets tired and therefore some rest is inevitable. The period or rest varies from spirit to spirit; but a normal spirit requires about 6 to 7 hours' rest at a stretch. Assuming that our average spirit had a rest of say 7 hours from 12 to 7, he is up at 7 A.M. He is of course not worried about the cares of the body, and the first thing a spirit does in the morning is to worship his deity or God. This is in a way obligatory on all spirits except the elementals, the idea being to make spirits healthy-minded.

This roughly takes an hour. After this, the ordinary spirit has no particular work and therefore there can be no routine similar for all. Some of them while away their time in talking among themselves, while there are some who feel delighted in moving about in their plane. Some, who have friends in other planes, go to them or call them; those who have appointments with mediums go to them. In this manner they spend their mornings. It is obvious that spirits who have special duties to perform at once attend to them from the morning. When the Court opens, many spirits go there and hear trials. The Court has long hours of work and spirits can go there at any time during the day, though the popular time is from 12 noon to 4 P.M. Over and above these ways of utilising the free time which spirits get, they usually devote their time to peace by resting in their particular plane. They do not keep themselves occupied for the whole day: yet spirits who are by their very nature industrious and active are always found busy and many of them go actually to the human world, especially in the evenings and afternoons. Perhaps this may sound a bit absurd. A spirit does not come down to the world when he desires to talk with a medium, and one may wonder why spirits should use their evenings in visiting the Earth; but the reason is quite clear; most spirits have finished their allotted tasks and the Court session being nearly at an end, it is very convenient to have a stroll then. Some spirits who have multifarious activities often find no time for such a migration and on the contrary, use it for attending to their mediums. At night time the principal activity is to give reports. Those who are engaged in the investigation department are busy during the early hours of the night; but the others who have done a good day's work rightly earn a good rest. Among the activities during the night time, lectures and stories form an important part, because out of so many spirits there are certain persons who come forward to deliver some lectures. Others who find their mind better suited to higher and intellectual topics, begin some friendly debates or discussions on various topics; while, those who are not inclined to tax their brains either with sedate lectures or controversial debates, take pleasure in the popular pastime of talking. This gives an idea of the routine day-to-day life of the spirit-identities and departures from this routine are rare indeed.

CHAPTER VII

THE BONDS WITH THE WORLD

Worldly Affections—Change of Sphere after Death—Influence of Planes on Temperament of Spirits—Condition of Feelings before Death—Mediums and Coldness of Spirits—Unfulfilled Desires— Shraddha and the Progress of Spirits—Blood-relations and Friends—Attraction at First Sight.

Worldly Affections

Human existence has its own charms spoken of as MAYA by the Indians or worldly bonds by the English-speaking people. These words, so far as I know, are used in such a way that their real meaning is obscure to us and the more we try to understand their significance the greater is the confusion caused. The situation created is not a happy one. Viewed from a practical point of view, it is nothing but the outcome of close and continued association with certain persons. Seeds of good relation are sown and the ultimate result is that we get ourselves so closely associated, attracted, and bound up that life without certain persons becomes next to impossible. In this way, I have tried to explain the origin of worldly bonds. It is however not certain whether these relationships are the result of accident or brought about in some other manner. To me it appears that the birth factor plays an increasingly important part and broadly speaking, worldly bonds are largely circumscribed by the conditions in which a particular soul is placed. At the same time, we should not ignore the factor of human design. At the present moment the circumstances are such that man tends to defy natural relationships and form other relations which cannot be regarded normal. To give you an example, in the western countries, we find that the collective ideal has been replaced by the individualistic ideal and the bonds of the joint family system are practically becoming things of the past. In eastern countries, however, the philosophy of individual welfare has not caught the public fancy to that extent and the old natural bonds are more or less still intact. Thus, a father loves his son even though he may be mature enough and considers it his duty to protect him still. In this way the bread-winner considers himself the pivot of the whole family and, for his whole life, labours hard to protect the members. In view however of the developments in modern times, it is evident that friends play a very important part in human attractions. Those people who are either not fortunate in having a family life or rather those who have a house but not a home are naturally found to be keenly interested in their friends. There are thus two types of bonds; one which arises on account of conditions of birth and the second one on account of relations which are formed by human efforts. But usually marriage forms a third type of bond, and it is a class by itself because we thereby turn a friend into a relative and the bond is different from the other two described before.

Change of Sphere after Death

Life in the world marks a stage only if we consider the aggregate life of a soul, both the mortal and spiritual together, because death does not mean an end of the person in the real sense. With this idea in our mind, we naturally feel anxious to know whether the soul keeps up its past relations. This is a point which has confused many brains and I am afraid no clear-cut reply is likely to be given in this book. But it can be safely asserted that death, even though it may not signify an end, does mark a very definite and a strong change in the soul's life. This change is better described by saying that after death, there is a change of sphere in the soul's life and this accounts for the fact that old bonds are not kept up and the soul has to leave the world completely. All the same, though it is not absolutely impossible to maintain the old relationships, it certainly does require a very strong degree of feelings to keep up some part of these even after death. In case of ordinary people, however, death casts a curtain over the past life severing all old connections.

Influence of Planes on Temperament of Spirits

Tracing further the analysis of human relations, we have to consider the part which different planes play in the life of spirits. In the first plane, we know that there are two type of spirits. Or these, the elementals have very strong relations with the world. This is possible because they have some more powers than other spirits; mediums also stand to gain for some time at least by establishing connections with them. Mutual advantage therefore strengthens the bonds between them. But these bonds are those after death and it is very doubtful whether these spirits care to strengthen their old relations. It is certainly true that if an opportunity occurs, they are very glad to meet their old friends or relatives and are ready to help them as far as it lies in their powers. Very often attempts are made by them to ask their dear ones to meet them. In this way, the bonds do not get effaced at least among the elementals. If we consider other class of spirits in this plane, they have not the brain power to form any relations and if these were formed, their desires being weak, they cannot remember anything of the past life. Worldly affections among the second class of the first plane-spirits are thus very loose and sentiment is absent in their lives.

In the second plane, or the Bhu Loka, we know that there are spirits who are below the average in their brain power but are a bit better than their counterpart in the Patala. Their desires are weak and their powers of attraction very little and few mediums care to talk with them. In this case, feelings do exist, but they are nearly dormant and only in exceptional cases, we find some satisfactory expression of feelings, though it must be noted that these spirits are not by their very nature, cold.

In the third plane, we have a class of spirits who represent the average or the middle class, and here we find the normal human bonds too. Most of the spirits are fairly intelligent, and have to a certain extent, developed independent thinking and have certain likes and dislikes. They are persons who always cherish the memories of their life in the world and are always fond of remembering their relatives and friends as far as it is possible to do so. But there is not that fervent desire which is found among the fifth-plane-spirits and the memory is, also, not strong. In this way, the spirits of the Tapa Loka are always found making an attempt to maintain a very close touch with the world and if they get suitable mediums, they are able to respond fairly well.

In the Chandra Loka, we find spirit who have had a successful life and therefore are found feeling happy about it. But, at the same time, the quality of ambition being not strong, they are satisfied with what they have achieved. As regards their feelings, they always have tried to be very calm and collected and therefore the expression which they give to them is so mild that some may consider them heartless, while others may class them as fatalists. I, for one, feel that their balanced nature is so closely associated with reason that feelings find no prominent place in their actions.

In the illustrious plane, which is called the Surya Loka, the all-pervading and guiding force is ambition. In psychological science, we are given to understand that the stronger the ambition, the greater the strength of feelings and with this dictum I agree completely. Among the spirits of this plane, we find therefore that feelings play a very important part in their lives. There is a fervent desire for progress and this in its turn leads them to create new bonds of affection; but their brain power being very strong, their memory is exceedingly sharp and the old bonds are not easily forgotten. Coldness is a quality unknown to them and they have very strong likes and dislikes. They have very good friends; but at the same time, they have an army of enemies too. Furthermore, most of them being somewhat connected with the administrative authorities, they find it very easy to get suitable mediums and this makes it possible for them to maintain the old associations. Their desire to meet people of the world should, however, on no account, be confounded with the similar desire of third-plane spirits, which are the desires of fondness not of ambition. Spirits of the Surya Loka are always keen on meeting people who are above the average or those who have achieved some success in the material world and this attitude on their part often invites unwarranted criticism of being regarded as either status- or intelligence-snobs; but, this is not true in so far as such an attitude is justified on account of the fact that the idea behind it is one of progress. It cannot be denied however that very often the old bonds have to be neglected on the ground of inferior status or brain power. But this is inevitable.

In the sixth stage of the spiritual ladder, we find that there is an apparently backward march, the Surya Loka denoting the climax. But this statement is far from the truth. It is however certain that in this stage bonds become very loose and the tendency of spirits is towards spiritual advancement, completely neglecting the material side. One of the striking features in this plane is coldness which is the dominating trait. All talk of past relationship is thus out of place; feelings do not play any important part in their lives. They are always eager to avoid people who would drag them to worldly desires. In this, nature seems to help them, for their memory also gets stable as it were and they very easily forget their past relatives and friends.

It would be presumptuous on my part to gauge the feelings of persons in the seventh stage who are god-like. Perhaps I do not possess enough powers to read their minds; but it is agreed on all hands that they are free from 'maya' or worldly temptations. I am afraid, however, 'maya' has its sway even upon them sometimes. Their feelings cannot find a suitable expression because mediums have either not the powers to call them or they have not got the necessary courage to face them. They speak very little and it is not proper for us to make surmises about these high souls.

Condition of Feelings before Death

During the life of every man, there are occasions which rouse his feelings; but in all cases the intensity is not the same; because every man has a different temperament. But death is such a unique incident that all people experience the same type of feelings irrespective of their nature. People, who in their life time may have even conceived a disgust for worldly life, never wish to leave the world. Even those who have renounced the world forget their philosophy of life and become purely material. Family ties and affections become absolutely fresh before the eyes of the dying person. His love and care for them become very strong and if he is surrounded by members of his or her family, the feelings are so strong that none but a dying person can realise them. Those who have many friends in the same way remember them with the same intensity of feelings. All this is very natural and yet one thing which one could desire is that God should have devised some method by which a dying person can overcome these feelings. It is absolutely necessary, because as it is the pain of death is very little, but for these intensified feelings. Even after the death of a particular person, such strong feelings continue to remain strong for some time. The pain of parting gradually diminishes and the horror or death being over, the soul gets cooler than before. He gets settled soon and is able to cope with the new situation easily and in a few days, normal feelings begin to guide this life. But the time taken to regain this normal position depends more upon the temperament of the person concerned rather than the nature of his death.

Mediums and Coldness of Spirits

The picture which is just put before you should make you believe that in the world of the dead, the chief quality is all pervading coldness. What is the reason? Perhaps, the explanation is that even among living persons such coldness does prevail and this should not be forgotten when we think of the feelings of the dead. Very frequently, it happens that people who call their relatives after their death expect them to be warmer than before. Perhaps, some persons will not agree but this is the expert psychological view. Now some feel that the only agency which can remove this coldness is that of the mediums. But I do not see any reason why mediums should bother about the feelings of their friends' or clients' relatives; and sometimes it may look indecent also. It is not possible to remove coldness if it is real; but the only thing which mediums can do it to acquaint their customers or friends with the facts which are already explained before, and also give a clear idea of the shortcomings of the spiritual talk. Very often the sitting appears cold on account of the fact that the visitor is not free in talking in the presence of strangers or he is not able to adapt himself to the new circumstances. In these conditions, a good medium by his powers of explanation makes the sitting more successful and to this extent, he can remove coldness.

Unfulfilled Desires

So far we have talked of the feelings of persons who had led a normal life which in a way can be regarded as successful. In such circumstances, most of the worldly desires are satisfied and in a way the person is ready to meet his end. But, in the imperfect human world, there are certain persons whose lives are not normal and they die at a time when they are not prepared to face the inevitable death. When they die, their mission of life remains unfulfilled and their desires unsatisfied. They are naturally most reluctant to leave the world. Moreover, if some of them meet with an unnatural death, the strenght of unfulfilled desires is extremely great. Sometimes when even everything is normal, a particular problem may be facing that person and this may create a state of unstable equilibrium for leaving the world. The complications or these abnormal circumstances are how ever not severe, inasmuch as in most cases, it is very difficult to procure a suitable agency to maintain the old relationship. Even if some of them can find a medium, that medium may not be in a position to bring about the reunion. Further, the dead person realising his or her inability to do anything towards the achievement of those objects assumes an air or contentment, and gradually their unfulfilled desires become a thing of the past, and the spirit begins to take interest in the new surroundings in which he resides. Further, people who die an unnatural death sometimes crave to go back to the world and for days together make serious attempts to do so; but in every case time is the best cure, and gradually these excited feelings cool down and normal conditions prevail. But the only significant fact about these abnormal cases is the after their death, they take some months to settle down and to this extent, they are regarded unhappy.

Shraddha and the Progress of Spirits*

Among the Hindus, there are certain ceremonies which a living person performs for the dead one to help him in his spiritual life. I am not a Hindu and therefore I do not know all the details about those ceremonies; but the outstanding among them is the Shraddha ceremony. It is the annual offering given to the dead so as to satisfy him, but in which respect the satisfaction is necessary is not made clear. But it seems to me that the original idea was to appease the departed person's unfulfilled desires by trying to satisfy some needy person in that direction. Thus, for example, in a case of a person whose chief attention was centred in eating good food the relatives try to satisfy that desire by feeding poor persons. In the light of the information available to the spirits, all have agreed that such actions do not in any way satisfy the unfulfilled desires of the dead, nor do they help their further progress. The only benefit which accrues to the dead is that he feels that his

---

* This paragraph was dictated by Sir Arthur in reply to an issue raised by me as to the possibility of actions on the part of the living doing good to the souls of the departed.

relatives have not totally forgotten him. At the same time, the living persons derive some satisfaction in trying to help their dear ones. But, if a person knowing all these facts continue to perform the old ceremonies, I am sure he is not getting an adequate return and the best way would be to discontinue such practices.

Blood-relations and Friends

The general genesis of bonds with the world has been discussed before. But most of you are perhaps anxious to know whether near relatives or properly speaking blood-relations take an active interest in the persons they have left behind and further, whether they attempt to better the prospects of their relatives in the living world. It must be stated that the spiritual planes have a very strong influence on the dead persons; but broadly speaking, blood relationships, like that of the father and the son, brother and sister, mother and son or daughter, are diffcult to be broken up at once and to dilute such feelings, there is the need of the time element which varies from one to five years according to the nature of the person concerned. But all these feelings are only fond affections which do not materialise into action. In case of friends, the whole problem depends upon the intimacy between them and if the bonds of friendship are so strong as to resemble blood-relationship, the above facts apply to them with equal force.

Attraction at First Sight

In almost all cases, we can find instances where a particular person feels that he should develop friendly relation with a person whom he has seen hardly for a few minutes and sometimes, the reverse feelings also spring up. In most cases, the other party shows a like response. What is the cause which can explain this attraction or repulsion at first sight? It has no spiritual background and the living persons should be able to analyse it. But if my analysis is correct, God has gifted us with the power of finding one's own level in the sense that we can at once make out a person's characteristics and we get attracted to those who resemble us. In a similar way, repulsion can be explained. Some may try to correlate these attractions and repulsions with past life's associations, but this is not true.

CHAPTER VIII

THE POWERS AND DISABILITIES OF SPIRITS

Mental Powers: General — Elementals and Haunting — Evil Consequences of Help from Elementals — Ordinary Spirits — Higher Spirits: Inspiration — Advice—Guesses about Future — Access to Divine Souls — Medium's Influence — Materialisation — Details of Next Birth — Attendance on Mediums — Vision — Production of Sound — Memory — Knowledge of Past Birth — Transmission of News — Boons — Spirits among Themselves — Impersonation and Misleading.

Mental Powers — General

In the preceding chapters, you must have seen that though spirits are deprived of their physical senses, they do retain their mental powers. It is natural that the spirit-identity which is a minor part of the whole soul cannot be expected to possess the same amount of ability and memory after death. The ebb is, however, not so marked and the identity faithfully retains much of the former ability and memory. Yet, in many cases, even a casual observer finds that detailed information cannot be obtained from the spirits; and an atmosphere of vagueness pervades spirit-communications. This tendency is all the more pronounced on account of the fact that mediums in general fail to translate all the information imparted by spirits. These are, in general the short-comings which affect the mental powers of all the spirits.

Elementals and Haunting

Some may include the elementals among the spirits. But I

have always regarded them as something different and for the purposes of this book, spirits do not cover these elementals. As we have seen before, these identities have more powers than average spirits. What are the causes which make them powerful is not known to most of the spirits and I also do not profess to know all the details about them. But, it is certain that, these souls somehow or other manage to retain full mental powers with a sharp memory. And, further, they can do certain things which persons with physical senses can only perform. I really do not know what powers act as such fine substitutes of physical powers. It may be that these persons while alive were exceptionally brilliant and had developed a strong and sturdy power, which seems to serve their purpose even after their death. It goes without saying that all their ability is misdirected and they prefer to use their powers to achieve things which a person with good and moral ideas would hate. In this manner, we see that elementals are quite distinct from spirits and our ignorance about such people is also pardonable because none of us would be willing to mix with them. We have often heard of people mistaking elementals for spirits and they loosely say that spirits can haunt. But, it should be made clear that spirits cannot and do not haunt, even though their desires are not satisfied. It is only an elemental who is capable of haunting, especially when his desires are not satisfied. Haunting has usually a bad odour, because it directly implies an element of injury to some person through the agency of the elemental. There cannot be haunting without a bad motive and these two facts are inseparable. Some of my mediums have often expressed their desire to meet an elemental; but the above facts being rigid, it is most inadvisable to do so.

Haunting may take various shapes. But, in any form, it is an act of the elemental which may be performed elemental is capable of coming down to the earth and being empowered to remove things or create various noises, he is able to frighten the person whom he desires to trouble. Further, he is in a position to materialise and this act of his is bound to give a very rude shock to the person who has the misforutune to come into contact with him. The feeling of revenge is so pronounced among the elementals that they go to the extent of troubling the person daily and bring about an end of life which however does not come soon, and as it were, death is spread over a few years.

Evil Consequences of Help from Elementals

The facts which I have stated just now have been known to people in some form or other; and they call the person who invokes such elementals as either a magician or a wicked person under the control of Satan as it were. Even in Indian mythology, this art was called wicked. Yet, all descriptions about the elementals tend to give us an idea of the enormous powers possessed by them. Even at the present time, you may come across persons who are directly in touch with very powerful elementals. Some of you may ask why should people aspire to be in touch with these elementals who in the end are bound to bring about their ruin. The reason lies in the fact that human nature is not generally able to resist the temptations which cross its path. The aid which an elemental can render is beyond description; no living person can get a clear idea about their powers and abilities, but it can be stated with confidence that they very often can perform things which neither human beings nor divine beings can normally do. To give you some idea of their powers, it may be mentioned here that they are able to bring about the death of any person they like. Further, obtaining of riches and wealth is also very easy for them. To bring information from distant places, which is not known, because of its being kept secret or otherwise, is also within their powers. The only thing that they cannot do is to change the other important incidents of either the medium's life or that of the person suggested by the medium. Thus, for example, if a medium who is in touch with an elemental is ill, no powers of the elemental can relieve him of the sufferings and to this extent, the powers of the elemental cannot be a substitute for divine powers. With the assistance of elementals every conceivable material prosperity can be secured; but the price would be too high in the end.

Ordinary Spirits

In some connection or the other, we have spoken about the average spirit. But here a few words may be added to complete the picture. When a person dies, he is shorn off all powers except the mental ones which even are not allowed to remain at their former level. But, more or less, these powers are not taken away. The popular idea is that the dead person's spirit after undergoing a change is better equipped with the powers of thinking, judging and prediction. But I will again repeat that they are just the same, not one ounce more than before, so far as the mental powers are concerned; and when the mind is deprived of the co-operation of other physical powers, it is very likely to be a bit inefficient in performance.

Higher Spirits: Inspiration

So far we have devoted our time to thinking about the powers of ordinary spirits. But when we think of spirits who have advanced both spiritually and mentally, we find that they are endowed with one very important power and that is of inspiring others. Many of the mediums think that all spirits in general should be able to inspire; but they are mistaken, insofar as it requires a very high degree of mental efficiency to perform the work properly and, furthermore, it necessitates a continued and a very powerful effort on the part of the spirit concerned. This seemingly easy work of inspiring is as a matter of fact a very difficult task. But spirits who are in the fifth plane or above are generally able to do so. It is recognised however on all hands that the desire to inspire springs only when the spirits' feelings are aroused. Thus, for example, if a particular soul is interested in some person living in the world, he can inspire him to perform a certain thing or to abstain from doing so. It very often happens that he may fail to inspire if all the circumstances are not favourable. The first requisite of successfully performing the work is that the party beyond the world of the dead should be efficient enough to catch the suggestions from the world beyond. Other spirits can also inspire, but they use their powers in few cases. In their case, the chance of failure is small. But some of you may feel that in the present state of spiritual development, there are mediums who can do the work better. But they fail to realise that the spirits can only talk when the mediums desire, while if they can inspire, the need of this intermediate agency is removed, and the spirits can communicate their ideas whenever they like. But I have told you before, the authorities here are not at all keen on such free and intimate relations being established between the two worlds.

Advice

It is natural that souls who advance further both spiritually and materially are equipped with high mental powers. They have a trained memory and in their various lives have faced problems which can be regarded as fairly complex and difficult of solution. In a word, they have seen the world completely and their mind is moulded by vast and rich experience. Naturally such spirits can judge things in a most rational way and keep their heads cool, while discussing even the most controversial points. Rashness and haste are not in their nature. Further, the power of analysis is so well developed that every problem set to them appears simple. These spirits when interested in either certain persons or certain topics can use their ability to a great extent and, thus, give very good advice to people on friendly terms with them. The great quality which is found in them is unbiased judgment and clear criticism

Guesses about Future

The popular idea of spirits knowing the future is wrong. But it may be said that some spirits do attempt to predict and that they are fairly successful. The explanation lies in the fact that though no predicting is possible, nearly correct guessing is not difficult under certain circumstances, the important factors being the high mental powers of the spirit, his experience in that direction, and his ability to remain unbiased. Most of the spirits of the Surya Loka are in a position to satisfy these conditions, but they are not ready to use their brains in things without any foundations, and it is difficult to get reliable spirits to use their powers in this particular direction. But there are some spirits who in their lighter moods do indulge in this interesting pastime and some of them, being really gifted with the above mentioned abilities, prove very useful to persons who by chance happen to call them. It must be remembered however that no great weight should be attached to what they say and the best way is to treat their words with caution and care.

Access to Divine Souls

Those high spirits are either in the fifth, sixth or the seventh plane and on account of the status they hold they enjoy certain privileges, the chief among which is permission to approach divine souls. The words "divine soul" do not include the Creator himself, but his representatives only. Thus, all these spirits can see the God of Death or the Yama Raj himself and other divinities, but not the all-pervading God. In case of spirits who are in the seventh stage and who are in awaiting salvation, an exception is made sometimes, though such incidents are very rare. As a matter of fact, I have often endeavoured to meet God himself, but I have never been successful so far. Even those who get an audience with God are never able to discuss anything, because. He never enters into any discussion and the period is so short that the spirit may at the most state his problem or grievance as the case may be. Be it said to the credit of Yama Raj however that he grants a free interview where there is no limitation of time and he is ready to prove his point. Other divinities are generally kind and they give a patient hearing though, in all these cases, redress of grievances, either personal or collective, is not common, because they, in general, maintain that the whole machinery is perfect and there should be no cause for complaint, and whatever appears to us as troubles is ascribed to the lack of correct realisation of the real situation. We are asked to believe that we have no reason to complain and that we must surrender ourselves before the mighty Soul who has no doubts about the wisdom of what is done either by Him or His agents. But, I beg to differ, even though I have the misfortune to differ from my Creator. I am, in a way, not free to give my reasons for differing from such a Great Authority nor have I definite proofs to establish the fact of imperfection that prevails here.

Medium's Influence

It has been an established fact that all spirits of the dead world of even seven planes can be invoked by mediums including the elementals even. Some of us think that when a particular spirit is invoked, he must come; this however is not correct, because after all friendly relationship depends on mutual willingness and if a spirit does not want to come, he can most easily defy a medium's call. The analogy of a telephone is correct here because it is just like receiving a call and then breaking off the connection. It is however true that nobody can prevent a medium from calling a spirit, but if we talk of normal circumstances, we find that most of the spirits are very keen to talk with mediums; on the contrary their desire to talk is not adequately satisfied. But I have seen spirits who are, by their nature, very reserved and feel very unhappy when they are made to talk. With some spirits the communal or the feeling of being say a European or an Indian is so strong that an Indian spirit does not like to respond to the call of an English medium and the converse is also true. The weaknesses of human nature are also present in the spirits and discrimination among mediums and spirits is therefore inavoidable to a large extent. But it may be stated that if a medium is of a tolerant disposition spirits of all kinds would like to meet him. Further, we find that nowadays better relationship exists between spirits and mediums of different nationalities.

Materialisation

In the Introduction we said something about materialisation and, if I mistake not, I have given you some rough idea of the whole phenomenon and it is no use repeating the same. It must be admitted that all spirits are not gifted with the power to materialise. Elementals, who are very powerful, are invariably successful in taking a shape; but other normal spirits are not able to condense the necessary vapour to take some concrete form. No particular plane is endowed with this power. But, in practically every 'loka', there are stray cases of spirits who can materialise; but, even among them, we find that they are not invariably successful in taking the form. Those spirits, who can materialise, are besides not in a position to take the same form every time and the spirit in the material form is not able to give out his identity. Thus, if the spirit of say Mr. X, were to materialise, he might not resemble the physical form of Mr. X and I would go a step further and say that the material shape may not resemble a physical human form and as a matter of fact the form has no clear-cut outline, and it is very difficult to give an idea of an ever-changing mass of vapour. Furthermore, some of the advanced spirits have even said that a real spirit should never desire to have any form and should constantly avoid materialisation. It is a sign of backwardness to hanker after a thing which shows that the spirit is not free from worldly desires, and is still a worshipper of Maya. The higher a soul rises, the weaker is the desire for any form. I have also thought over these words very often. If examples were to be considered correct, it is a fact that low-bred spirits or unhappy spirits usually materialise; a good and a noble spirit does not care to do so. My line of argument is not on the desirability or otherwise, but on ability or otherwise. A powerful spirit, if he wants to show his ability to materialise, should be able to do so; but as the matter stands, even fairly powerful spirits fail to do so in spite of very strong desires to achieve those powers. When

I was discussing this point with Yama Raj, he told me that materialisation was a degrading phenomenon for a Surya Loka spirit and he advised me to think of the final merger and to abandon all ideas of individual existence. My point still centres round the inability of good spirits to take a form even for the sake of convincing the people in the world of the living of the existence of spirits. But it is no use thinking of a thing which is considered undesirable from the point of view of both material and spiritual progress. I also feel that the God of Death is correct in the view he holds about materialisation.

Details of Next Birth

In various seances, you must have experienced that all spirits are very reluctant to disclose any information about the birth which they have taken and some of you, I am sure, must have resented such an attitude on their part. But the reason is not far to seek. Every spirit is ordered by the Court authorities not to disclose material facts about the new or current births. The word 'material' is very vague. But if my interpretation is correct, it means that the information disclosed should be adequate or definite enough to give out the full particulars of the new birth. Supposing, by any chance, the details given suffice to trace the dead person in his new birth, such a person is said to have broken the divine command, and the person dies at once as a penalty for breach of promise and has to stagnate in the same plane for nearly ten births. This is the punishment so far as the spirit is concerned. But the medium tempting to elicit the information has to suffer, not while on the world of the living, but when facing the Final Trial. I therefore advise my mediums not to try this harmful experiment. You must be all the while wondering why the authorities do not desire such facts to come out. But the restriction exists for very good reasons. Suppose, a relative of a person is dead and he discloses his next birth. The living person then tries to trace him in his new garb and, all the while considers him as his relative and bonds of affection grow up, and if this were allowed, the circle of near relatives would expand like a spiral spring, the complications of our domestic life would have no end, and human life would indeed be a burden. If you can visualise such a society, perpetually increasing its relatives and friends, I am sure, you would advocate the same restrictions which are laid down by the Court. It is primarily for the safety and happiness of ourselves that divine authorities have kept the new birth a closed book.

Attendance on Mediums

It has been explained in connection with various topics that the divine authorities have never objected to spirits attending the mediums. But, at the same time, I must admit that such meetings and calls have never been encouraged even for advanced spirits. This might appear to you very strange; but references to such an attitude on the part of the divine authorities have been given in ancient works about spiritualism in India. This is evidenced by the fact that some religious Hindus do not consider it proper to call their departed relatives or friends. But persons in the world should not think for a moment that divine authorities are absolutely against it, because if such were the case the powers to call spirits would not have been given. Their point of view is that if spirits were to develop a very strong contact, it would result in a dual existence, which from various points of view is not desirable. Thus, spiritualism practised with moderation and caution does meet with the approval of divine authorities.

Vision

Every fortunate human being is endowed with the power of sight; but the importance of sight is never fully realised except by few who are deprived of this precious gift. This commonplace power of vision is not so common in the world beyond. The reasons are obvious, because all the physical senses cease to exist and whatever powers are there emerge out of the brain. As we have seen in the preceding pages, the mental faculty is very unevenly distributed among the people created and most of the spirits are not able to visualise through their brain. Only a select few who are fortunate in transcribing vision through a very strong brain are able to see partly. It may be made clear here however that spirits can make use of the human agency for the purpose of seeing and a spirit finds no difficulty in seeing through an efficient medium. This is possible on account of the fact that the spirits can make use of the human eyes. I for one feel there should have been a better provision made for seeing than the one in existence, because if there is one great trouble in the spirit world, it is this. But at the same time, I do realise that without any physical senses, it is difficult to give this power, though for gods no barriers are insurmountable.

Production of Sound

Here also I have to repeat the same old story, because most of the spirits are not in a position to create any sound, nor can they utter a word. It will appear to you very strange that we cannot talk in the normal way; but we are gifted with a special power to convey our thoughts quickly and efficiently to other spirits and mediums. The accuracy of facts conveyed is in no way impaired and I might go a step further and say that perhaps it is a better method than speech, because speeches have to be couched in phrases while thoughts can be sent without such trouble. So much for talking. But as regards production of sound, the spirit is not in a position to create any sound nor does any substitute exist for it. I had a talk with the God of Death and he in his usual way said that we never need that power, and I agree with him, because the nature of our duties or the pleasures in which we indulge are so designed that production of sound has no place in out system of life. Furthermore, Yama told me that the world which spirits leave for some time is full of every type of sound and there is no need to pollute the divine atmosphere which is devoid of any kind of disturbance. But my argument centres round the inability and not the undesirability of the spirits to create any sound. As the matters stand, however, there is no way out of it. At this point, it must be made clear that spirits can create sound through their mediums and the most common example is found in planchettes and even to a smaller extent, in the Ouija Boards, because some sound is produced. The elementals however do possess this power and this is often proved when they make noise by tampering with our furniture and such other small pieces. Production of sound is thus not rare but totally absent, so far as the spirits of the dead world are concerned, barring the elementals. Some mediums have requested spirits to create sounds to prove their existence; but I am sure they are ignorant of the above facts.

Memory

In this book, great importance has been given to the mental factor, both in the case of human beings and spirits and it has often been said that spirits possess the same mental powers. But this is not absolutely true, because in certain respects the abilities of the spirit and the living person differ. It was my constant endeavour to find the cause and in the light of my present knowledge it appears that the mind of the spirit is weaker than the soul's because the spirit mind works in isolation so far as the physical senses are concerned. It is a fact that other qualities of the mind do not depreciate to a large extent; but the faculty of memory is considerably weakened. Memory stands in a special class by itself and that too with a good reason. It is obvious that if a person were to remember incidents of lives after lives, his mental stability would be lost and cumulative effects of various sad and painful incidents would be absolutely unbearable for the delicate thinking instrument, the mind. To keep our lives free from these troubles, God has thought it fit to weaken the memory after one dies. Memory does not remain permanently weak however because as soon as the person is reborn, the mind regains its full form.

Knowledge of Past Birth

In the preceding paragraph, we have seen how the power of remembering diminishes and the actual result of the said effect is seen when we find that the spirit after some time gradually forgets the life he had led before. This process is not very quick and it takes a fairly long time to efface all the detailed information of the past life. But at the same time, my readers must be aware of the fact that soon after the death of a person, the sphere of life is changed and there is a definite break in the whole system of memory. But hazy and vague ideas persist for nearly twenty years, and this accounts for the fact that most of our dead friends or relatives are in a position to remember something and are certainly in a position to recollect what the living people say. The idea behind the short-lived memory is already explained before. I have always viewed this problem from a different stand-point, because I feel that when a person is made to forget the incidents of prime importance in his life, he naturally forgets the experience he had gained and the price paid for not recollecting sad incidents of past lives is too heavy. The soul like a rolling stone gathers no moss; but the authorities maintain that the evolutionary effect upon the soul is never effaced, and the impressions for all purposes are permanent. I am not in a position to verify the validity of the argument; but in view of the absence of further details they may be considered nearer truth. We thus see that spirits are not in a position to remember very clearly and precisely all the incidents of their past life. Furthermore, the names of various relatives also are quickly forgotten and this state of affairs is accentuated by the inability of even the best of mediums to give proper expression to such names. It is rare to find a spirit who has such a strong memory as to enable him to express the names very correctly. It is true that these facts make proofs of the existence of spirits very difficult and more weight has to be placed on the general mode of talking to bring conviction of the genuineness of spirit-communication.

Transmission of News

In view of the powers of the spirits mentioned above, it is very natural to expect them to convey messages between various mediums, and to other spirits. Coming to actual facts however we find that the work is not so easy as it seems; but, at the same time, such transmission of news is certainly feasible. Thus, a good spirit from an efficient medium can carry the news to another medium of equal merit; but in practice, such conditions are not to be found, either one of the mediums or both are not efficient or the spirit does not possess the necessary ability or the conditions in which the spirit is called are not normal. Over and above these facts, the element of time which lapses between the two sittings is of considerable importance. This should suffice to explain the impediments which lie in the path of successful transmission of messages. Similar conditions obtain in the case of messages to be sent to spirits. But the distinction lies in the fact that only one medium is to be used; and to that extent, the task is easier. The spirit is not at the mercy of the medium, for thoughts can be passed between them at once; while in the other case, the transmission of the message depends upon the sweet will of the other medium.

Boons

We hear a lot about the boons which gods and goddesses are supposed to confer on various souls. To a large extent these divinities are in a position to confer such boons and favours; but it is not in the hands of spirits of all classes to give boons. It should not be thought however that spirits are not in a position to help others because those spirits who are in touch with divine souls can make requests to them to favour a particular soul. Thus, an indirect method of conferring favours does exist. But, in practice, such methods are not in use, and spirits are not in a position to help other souls in any way. This is naturally correct, because spirits are in no way better than living persons and we all know that human beings are not able to give any boons. Some of you may refer to ancient Hindu mythology where we come across various incidents in which saints and such other spiritually advanced persons are supposed to have either given a boon or a curse; but to me it appears that those persons must have expressed such desire and in a few cases, purely by accident, these boons or curses may have proved correct; but such results can never be brought about by human or spiritual design.

Spirits among Themselves

All the while we are talking about the various activities of the spirits and it is desirable to know their way of living among themselves. Barring relatives for the time being, the identities of numerous souls live in perfect harmony and peace. Their relations are absolutely normal and friendly. Such happy conditions exist only when they have had no personal knowledge of each other before their death, so far as their past life is concerned. But in the case of those spirits who knew each other before their death, the conditions are not so ideal. The same human weaknesses prevail there and all the good and bad qualities are to be seen. In short, the behaviour of spirits is just the same and friendship or enmity is the result. All this depends upon various other factors and no definite causes can be given. I am sure you must have got adequate proof of this side of the spirit life in the course of various sittings.

Coming to relatives, we find that the past bonds are revived and for some time at least their behaviour is such that the natural relationship can be clearly seen. In this case, as in many other cases, the element of time plays a very important part. But as a general conclusion it may be stated that their relationship is very similar to that of human beings and the general atmosphere is smoother on account of the fact that there are few things in which conflict of interests arises.

Impersonation and Misleading

This point is of considerable importance to the people in the world of the living, rather than to the spirits, because the system of communication is such that spirits can impersonate other spirits if they care to do so. Such impersonation often passes undetected and the person concerned is naturally misled, if not deceived. Some may argue that there is no reason to have such an apprehension; but spirits who have considerable free time at their disposal are very often tempted to go to a medium for a chat and this is to some extent natural. Even higher spirits of the fifth plane are found to be playing this game. There is so far no effective check in existence and we have to rely on the strength of the spirit invoked; because if he is powerful, he will be able to displace the spirit who is attempting to impersonate him. But if he is weak, then the practical joke becomes successful. From what I have gathered there are only a few cases in which such impersonation takes place; but very often it is the medium's spirit who in his keenness to make the sitting successful cheats his medium's customer or visitor. Such misleading is carried on on a large scale without the mediums knowing it.

CHAPTER IX

THE FINAL GOAL

Aim of Life in Worldly Sense—Idea of Karma—Reincarnation—Ambition—Moksha—Merger, the Peculiar End—Longevity of Life—God—Form—Residence— Powers— Darshan—Relation to other Gods—The Creator vs. Yama—Final Influence over the World—Purpose of Creation.

Aim of Life in Worldly Sense

In the preceding chapters, we have tried to give some idea about the life after death and in a way the book is complete; but it is in the fitness of things that some idea of the final goal should be given in the pages to follow. It is rather difficult to say anything definite about the aim of life either in a worldly sense or in the spiritual one, though the latter is less complex. Regarding the worldly aim of life it must be admitted that various people hold divergent views; but if we keep in mind the general class of people or to put it in other words, the materialist class, we find that their aim centres round the idea of self-betterment. They in the first instance want to become happy themselves and then to make their families happy. They seldom think of the life beyond death though they might have some vague notions about it. Salvation or merger is not their final goal, and they never seek to make any special effort to gain it. Still however we know that most of these people do worship God and pray to Him, not to advance them spiritually, but to redress their unhappiness in this very world. This is one class of aim of life if we bear in mind very broad classifications.

Then there are other sets of people who, as it were, do not

care much for the help of God and generally do not believe in worship. Their belief is that the Karma theory is the only correct one and they try to achieve their advancement by leading a good and productive life and thereby earn a good subsequent birth. In this belief, I find that there is nothing wrong if one expects a reward for what he has done, though better results may be achieved if such people have some respect for the Divine Authority. Even this class of people does not seem to covet the Merger though at the same time, they wish to advance themselves spiritually.

The third class of people in this classification is that of those who do not take any active interest in the world in which they are living. Their ideas of life are rather different. They take the world as a trap or *maya* and no effort is spared to avoid this material contact. Material advancement either of themselves or of their families or of the world is not their aim. They are mad after salvation and births and deaths are regarded as a great nuisance. I for one, feel that when we are sent to the world, the world should not be regarded as a trap and we must understand that we are expected to do our best in whatever sphere of life we are placed. At the same time, spiritual advancement should not be lost sight of because we must not forget for a moment that spiritual and material advancements are interrelated and neglect of one of the two is sure to affect the general progress.

Idea of Karma

In this way we come to the conclusion that Karma is the main thing, so far as the activities in the world of the living are concerned. Coming to Karma or deeds, we know that when we are judged in the Court, a detailed analysis is made of all the activities which we have carried on during our lifetime. It is not necessary to recapitulate the classification which I gave in the earlier part of this book. But one thing should be said that only very important acts performed by us have a bearing on our future development and the minor acts are of no consequence. Furthermore, it is agreed on all hands that good actions only do not earn a reward and the divine authorities expect some sort of worship for future spiritual progress. Material advancement can be secured without any worship, because there the divine authorities have no right to raise any objection on that ground. From this, it must be apparent that the theory of Karma is of greater value in securing material advancement, while in the case of spiritual one, worship has also some value.

Reincarnation

It is assumed that my readers have grasped the theory of reincarnation and it is now desirable to discuss the advantages and drawbacks of the actual position. Those of you who are not inclined to pin your faith in that theory may leave this point aside. Births and deaths are recurring phenomena and the natural question which arises in this connection is: Is it a desirable thing? Most people consider them to be a great source of trouble, while some consider them as training ground for material and spiritual progress. There are some who regard this mortal world as the real world and therefore they naturally cherish the idea of rebirths. My ideas on the subject are as under: I too believe that the human world is the real world so far as the individual existence is concerned. The spirit-world is the resting place for those of us who secure salvation. There exists a false notion about our permanent home, and we are led to believe that the spirit-world is the permanent home. If there were no births and deaths, we would not be able to get adequate experience and a change of sphere would be impossible. We clearly see therefore the utility of rebirths and there is no reason to develop a distaste for this very natural thing.

Ambition

Taking rebirth as a reality, we have to consider the main force which should guide our activities in various births. This world affords an excellent training ground and we are expected to prove that we want to progress further and further. Very often, contentment is considered as the best quality which a human being should acquire for spiritual advancement. This is a point however on which many people have expressed different opinions. Taking a rational view it must be admitted that contentment means slackening of our activities and it would not be in our interests to practise it in the earlier part of our aggregate life, that is, from the first birth till salvation. In that period the soul should bubble forth with ambition to progress and that too both materially and spiritually. At the same time, I agree that ambition also has limits. After, say, getting into the fifth plane or Surya Loka, there is nothing wrong if that feeling gradually cools down, and perhaps at that stage contentment may be a useful method of earning salvation. In a word, for individual existence, ambition is the only quality which can prove useful, but when that desire for individual existence changes into a desire for mixed existence with the Supreme Being, contentment is one of the methods. I have seen cases in which contentment was never practised and yet salvation was earned, though delayed by a few years. We can, therefore, stick neither to ambition nor to contentment and no one dictum can be invariably true.

Moksha

In this book, we have been talking about salvation or Moksha very frequently and yet no exact idea of that state of a soul has been given. In a way, I am not a suitable spirit for the purpose of defining Moksha, as I have not attained that stage. But, from what I know, it is a status conferred on those souls who have taken an adequate number of births, have secured the necessary experience and have progressed both materially and spiritually, the former in the earlier part of life and the latter in the later part. Further such salvation is not possible if there is a lurking desire for individual existence. A spirit satisfying the above conditions, over and above the necessary worship, can attain salvation.

Worship is a vague expression and I have failed to make out what type of devotion constitutes the necessary amount of worship. Naturally, it cannot be another word for flattery. At the most, it may be an appreciation of the qualities which the Supreme Being possesses or it may be deemed necessary to pay our respects and homage to the Almighty. The current forms of worship have very often neglected this real form of devotion and have made it a by-word for flattery and gods are alleged to reward those of us who flatter them. Indian mythology is replete with such apparent instances; but there we are confounding devotion with flattery. Anyway, it is certain that, without true devotion, salvation is not easy, as after all salvation is a sort of appreciation of the qualities of a soul.

Merger, the Peculiar End

Merger or salvation is the final stage in the natural evolution of a soul. It is a promotion from the seventh stage or the Deva Loka. But, one thing that distinguishes merger from other stages of evolution is that it puts to an end the individual existence. It relieves the soul who gets salvation from the trouble of births and deaths, if it is a trouble at all. Further it shows that you have stood the test of life creditably and you are fit enough to be merged with God, and thereby become one with Him. But, what we feel is that after attaining this development of mind and after securing such rich experience, we are lost to the world we have served so well. A soul who has led such an active life for years has to lead a life which knows no activities, though the Supreme Being is, no doubt, active. Is it not then peculiar that many of us covet this peculiar end? I for one feel that even if I were to be given salvation, I would be most tempted to decline the offer. Looking at the other side of the question, some hold that in our everyday life, after some years of hard eventful career, we need retirement and we do not grumble about a life of complete inactivity. By the same reasoning, applied in a broader sense, births and deaths too prove strenuous for a soul and naturally after some long years of this activity the soul should earn some rest, and it retires, as it were. But this retirement is not eternal, and this statement will be substantiated in the subsequent pages. I do not see any flaw in this reasoning, as such. Perhaps like most young men, I do not dream of retirement.

Longevity of Life

Material people never think of merger or salvation, and even though they possess some knowledge of the theory of reincarnation, they are very reluctant to leave the body. This feeling is absolutely true, and in a way, in the earlier part of the aggregate life there should be a strong desire to live a long life. It is true that when a soul is born, the span of life is determined in the court; but it is not an exact number of years, but a limit is set, something like fifty to seventy years. During those intermediate twenty years, the soul may be forced to leave the body; but it is in the hands of the soul to avoid moments of weakness in which death may overpower the soul. Moreover the mission of life also plays an important role and the longer you delay the fulfilment of those missions, the longer you live, and it is also to our advantage to have more than one mission of life, because then only it becomes difficult to fulfil all of them. These are the factors which have nothing to do with the physical body as such. Still however it should be stated that the soul has to take help from the body and therefore a healthy body is necessary for a long life. Thus a sound mind in a sound body avoids many moments of mental and physical weaknesses and thereby takes advantage of the full lease of life. If is not necessary to give some ideas about the methods of maintaining good health as it is a matter out of my sphere. It thus appears that to make use of the full span of life is easy; but the actual facts make us feel the other way, as, in most cases, the conditions laid down are difficult to abide by. At the same time, there are instances in which we find that full advantage is taken by the souls concerned.

From ages there is a lurking desire in human minds to conquer death. But everyone, when dying, feels that such an attempt proves futile, Death is a thing which can be delayed during the period allowed by the Court, as explained before. But further than that is beyond the human range. According to my knowledge it is not possible to postpone it and attempts made to defy it are always fruitless. It does not mean however, that we should surrender at once, because what we may take as death may turn out to be a moment of either mental or physical weakness, and it is in our powers to avert that crisis. In Indian mythology we find instances of certain persons having been made immortal. But I have found that such a boon would never be conferred on a soul in this world insofar as the ordinary human body is so made that it can roughly last for 150 years, and not more than that. Thus, the grant of immortality is a flight of imagination of some Hindu writers. It is a reality in the spirit-world, because every soul is immortal. Rewards however for special service or extreme devotion are sometimes given and if boons are given for lengthening life the decision of the Court can be changed. It may be added that Yama Raj has equal powers and therefore the Creator even cannot grant such a boon without his consent.

God

The great mystery is no longer a mystery for us. But every thing in the spirit world is capable of being explained except one thing and that is the Great Soul or the Supreme Being. From the very inception of this world we humans have always assumed that there is the Almighty God and that He has created the world or in a wider sense, the Universe and that He guides, controls and supervises each and every activity performed by millions of His sons and daughters. This idea of this extra-cosmic Being is still held by all of us. He is given various names in various countries and He is said to possess numerous qualities and virtues. But none of us has ever seen Him nor any exact idea of this Soul has ever been given. Yet the world is ruled by Him for centuries and it will be ruled for millions of centuries without we people getting even the faintest idea of Him. In these circumstances, I begin to describe Him in my own way with considerable diffidence and I am sure my readers will be broad-minded enough to overlook my inability to do justice to it.

Form

Various authors have attempted to conceive some form for this Great Soul, but I definitely know that like every other soul, He has no form whatever, and in this connection, I may add that this Soul, being composed of many souls which we possess, is only a spark of energy and that there is no matter. Yet, we must not forget that God, being able to give physical forms to so many of His parts, can very easily assume any form He desires. Indian mythology gives stray examples of God having taken form and staying on our earth for a number of years, and I think it is a valid statement. Similarly in other countries too, He may have actually come down, if not wholly, at least partially, and prophets of various religions are cases in point. But these instances should not lead you understand that He always assumes a physical form. Years may roll on without any form being assumed by Him and according to the reliable information which I have sought to procure, He should be regarded as one who assumes no physical form in normal circumstances.

Residence

God is supposed to reside in each and every corner of the whole universe created by Him. But it is natural for us to inquire where He normally resides. I myself have had no occasion to see this Supreme God and I cannot say where He exactly stays. But from my talks with Yama Raj, it appears that he is usually found in the seventh plane, that is, the Deva Loka. With big persons, we associate splendid palaces to live in, a magnificent city, but our God is found sharing the same position as the spirits of the Deva Loka. In respect of the problem of residence, He has reserved a big space for His own purpose and there He stay with His personal attendants. He has also a sort of a court, not for deciding cases as the God of Death does, but to hear appeals for mercy and for carrying on the work of creation. He is in a way residing in every nook and corner in so far as He has powers to see and know what is happening all over the world and this is true insofar as every part of the Soul goes to the world by rotation in the shape of fragmented souls, which take birth in the world.

Powers

Where there is a limit, there can be an analysis of powers. But in this case, there being no limit, there is as a matter of fact no need to enumerate the powers possessed by Him. Yet, to name a few of the many possessed by Him, He has full powers of creation, and there is no higher authority in this respect, though He generally consults the God of Death, in determining the broad policy to be followed. As regards the work of destruction, He has no powers. Even if He is angry with a particular soul, it is not in His hands to deprive him of his life. He, in that case, seeks help from Yama Raj. Taking the sphere of general administration of both the spirit-world and the human world, He has complete control and in discharging His duties. He has arranged such a method of distributing the work that only very important questions come up before Him. In this way, He administers the world, as is the case with our human governments. He possesses many special powers of mercy; He can grant a new lease of life or grant a special promotion in the advancement of a soul; He can improve the status of a particular soul in the world, He may merge a soul either when it proves too bad for the world or He thinks that it is deserving of such a high position. It may appear strange that God is not expected to prove what He feels about a particular soul, and He unlike Yama Raj can take arbitrary action. Here it appears that He is more absolute than Yama. It is not desirable to enlarge upon the usual powers which are common among higher souls. But one most important power is the one of knowing the future and the past also. He has no limitations of physical senses which spirits have in the spirit-world.

Darshan

This Supreme Being is endowed with the special power of taking form at any moment and therefore He can give a physical 'darshan' whenever He desires. But, such an opportunity is given only to those who are very much devoted to Him and that too after a protracted period of worship. Among the Hindus, there is a belief current that penance for a long time is bound to result in making God take a physical form. I do not definitely know how far this is true; but it is feasible no doubt. But I may make one thing clear and that is that a person who can secure such a concrete vision of God does not necessarily get salvation or get a very good birth. Yet a soul who can induce Him to come down is generally a high soul and hence the correlation of the two facts. I wonder whether it is in our interests to, as it were, sacrifice the whole of our life for that 'darshan'. Some say that is the best and noblest moment of life, not of one birth but all the 84 lacs, as it were. But I myself do not fancy this idea, because our mission of life is to prove useful to the world and not to satisfy this personal desire.

Relation to other Gods

In the preceding paragraph, we have seen that there is a definite system of government. The heads of the different departments and of different planes are all divine beings and are termed gods. Even controllers of different elements are called gods too. Curiously enough, Hindu mythology is full of such names and it is nearly confusing to analyse those long descriptions of various gods. I feel there is much of imagination rather than actual substance because they have been in the first place given physical form which is not true. Moreover the names given are also not invariably true and their powers unduly exaggerated. Coming to the relations of the Supreme God and these gods, one thing is clear and that is that all of them are subordinates so far as He is concerned except the God of Death, who is His equal. All these gods have to carry on the work of administration under His instructions and, even in minor details, they have to be very careful lest they may deviate from the rules laid down by Him. Thus, contrary to normal opinion small gods are not vested with any powers of their own and they are merely agents of the one Supreme Being. It may be added that all of them have the power to ask for an audience with the Almighty and there they can talk about matters concerning their sphere of work, and can suggest whatever they want to do. But in no case can they deviate, once a particular policy is laid down. Special powers can be granted to those of these divine beings, who are found worthy of such recognition of their services. Similarly, those who are unfit can be punished either by reducing their powers or by depriving them of their separate existence, by merging them, for some time or if need be, for a very long time.

There is a Hindu belief that there are some 33 crores of gods and there is over them a sort of a cabinet of three important gods namely of Shiva, Vishnu and Brahma. I do not believe in terminology, but there is a cabinet of three gods certainly viz. the God of Death or the Destructor, and the Supreme Being or the Creator and the general administrator known as Vishnu. We may regard Shiva as the God of Death and Brahma as the Supreme Being. But leaving aside these Indian names, the three important functions of the Universe are represented in this final cabinet. The functions of this body are mainly of a deliberative and advisory nature. Without such meeting of these three gods, it would not be possible to carry on the world properly. The work of creation and destruction has to be carried on in such great harmony that co-operation between the three is almost imperative. We have talked about gods and in this connection I may state that there are goddesses too. They also like gods work in the general system of administration, and enjoy equal powers with gods. There is one point which strikes us that when in the spirit-world no sex distinction exists, there is no reason to have goddesses. I am not in a position to clear the point. But, it appears that, certain souls who have been raised to this divine status had more female births than male ones and hence this female name attached to them.

The Creator vs. Yama

The Creator or the Supreme God and Yama or the God of Death are the two most important beings in the whole system of government and it is desirable to consider their relationship and their individual powers. It may be remarked that the importance of the God of Death is underestimated to a large extent and even the Hindus who worship all possible divinities have neglected him. His position is never recognised by us and it is high time that we should realise the true situation. The great powers of Yama Raj are alone adequate to show the very important position, he enjoys in the spirit-world. He is supreme in deciding the policy regarding destruction and even promotion to a higher stage is dependent on his ruling. While giving new birth, he is the person who determines what type of birth to give and such other allied things. The Creator who has vast powers regarding creation and over all other spheres of human life does not keep all the powers in His hands but delegates the control to His subordinates. It is curious to note that God, who has complete control of everything, has thought fit to take away all control from over Yama and He does not control, guide or supervise proceedings in Yama's Court. Yama thus in reality is an equal and not a subordinate. If these two powerful Souls were to work in isolation the whole Universe would come to an end. There is therefore a great need for a joint policy of work for these two Souls. The relations between the Creator and Yama are generally very smooth and cordial and they always take an important step after consulting each other. Occasions of important differences of opinion are very rare and in case such a sharp difference of opinion becomes rigid, Vishnu is supposed to pacify the parties concerned by His ready powers of bringing about a compromise.

Final Influence over the World

The above facts may lead you to believe that the Creator is not as powerful as He is depicted to be. But this is an illusion insofar as He does carry on the work of creation, destruction and administration through His two very powerful agents. Do not for a moment think that Vishnu and Yama are any different Souls than His own. After all, the Creator, God, is the Trinity Himself, and all these separate influences of the Three Big Souls emerge out of the one God. His influence on the world is far-reaching and very wide. It may perhaps appear that events can take place either without His knowledge or consent. But it must be realised that even the slightest movement in the Universe is according to His intentions. His control is absolute and the world moves on through the element of time and will go on for years together until the Creator thinks of taking away all His fragment of energy from the world.

Purpose of Creation

This is the last mystery which I am going to solve before I complete this work. It is extremely difficult to say how the world or the Universe came into existence, nor is it in my hands to tell you how the Great Soul or the Big Energy came into being. In other words, the birth of the Energy or Matter is a complete mystery to me and perhaps to all others including the gods whom I have had occasion to meet. It is a matter of regret that this important problem should have remained unsolved and that there should not be any prospects of finding out a solution. The only way to explain the purpose of creation is to assume that somehow this Energy was in existence and a part of this Energy was converted into matter. After this stage of development, the work of creation started. The mass of Energy could not remain idle and therefore fragments which emerged from it, took the shape of living beings and in this book, we are concerned with one type of them, namely the human beings. This is the only way in which this world of ours could have come into existence.

Taking the above assumptions as correct, we will examine the purposes underlying the continuous work of Creation. It is a well-known fact that souls who are born are expected to gain experience and to earn a retirement from active life or what is called a merger. But one does not understand why there should be no end to the work of creation. The Creator does not rest satisfied after His whole energy has been sent to the world in fragments. The reason is not clear nor is it explained by Him but what appears to me is as under: We assume that the Creator is composed of half the original energy and the other half is fragmented into various souls and they are in the world. As time passes, some of them get merged and if that process were to continue, in a number of years, the world would be devoid of life and again there would be Energy and Matter. There would be thus no sense in creating the world if God were to do this. It is also believed in authoritative circles here that if the Energy were to be devoid of any contact with the world, there could be no effective touch or link and this continuous chain of creation and merger maintains that necessary link. It may strike us to inquire why this Energy should be so active all these years. Is it not an ideal state of affairs to go back again to the point of starting; that is to say, make the Universe static? But may I remind you that everything in our world, either material or spiritual, is essentially dynamic?

Before I conclude this small book, I would be most ungrateful if I were not to thank very sincerely Diwan Bahadur Kaji and his son and nephew for the extremely cordial support and help which they have given me in bringing out this book. Without their assistance, my first hand knowledge would have remained absolutely obscure. Special mention should be made about their readiness to suit my odd and rigid demands regarding the time for writing the book. It is a great sacrifice on their part to have undertaken this work in its true sense of PURE SERVICE and I wish their efforts are appreciated by the public.

INDEX

A

Absent-mindedness 3
Acid 5
Activity 39, 56
—of spirits 35
Administrative work 48
Advice 103
Affections 89
Age 1
Agency 61
Agonised shrieks 2
Agony 2
Aid 6
Aim of life 115
Aimless existence 69
Almighty 119, 125
—God 121
Ambition 47, 117
Ambitious spirits 47
Arthur Conan Doyle, Sir 3, 42, 51, 96
Attendance at trials 42, 78
—on gods 81
—on mediums 108
Attendants 15
Automatic writing xxxii
Average spirits 100

B

Bad actions 22
—treatment 9
Balance of justice 19
—of power 19
Baser soul 20
Bhu loka 38-40, 91
Bird's eye view 41
Birth-s 1, 62
Birth full 65
—order 27
Blindfolded 7
Blood-relations 97
Bodily existence 4
Body 6
Boons 112-113
Brahma 125
Brain 52, 67
—power 77, 91
Buddha 60-61
Buddhist Doctrine 60
Bundles of goods 5
Burial 4

C

Calls of mediums 4
Captives 16
Captivity 3-4, 9
Carriage 7
Ceremony 4
Chain of births and deaths 60
Chandra Loka 44, 46, 47, 92
Change of sex 73
—of sphere 90
Chief justice 14, 16
Christ 60
Christians 59
Circumstances 62
Climbing 7
Cold Spirits 52
Coldness of spirits 94
Collective actions 43

Comfortable birth 64
Communication xxxvi
—with living 83
Concentration xxxvi
Condition of feelings 94
Conscious 3
Consciousness 2
Conscription 2
Control 7, 42
Conversation xxxii
Counsel 15
Court-s 14-16, 18, 20, 23, 34, 36, 79, 82, 86, 107, 116, 121
—trials 79
Creation 76, 127-128
Creator 34, 41, 61, 64, 76, 84, 105, 121, 126-128
Cremation 4
Crystal-gazing xxxiii
Curse 113

D

Daily routine 85
Death 1, 4, 62, 90-91, 113, 121
—messenger 2
—ray 2-4, 17
Deed-s 6, 60
Defence 25
Deity 32
Delays 18
Density of population 44
—of the air 13
Desire to respond xxxii
Desired spirit xxxiv
Destruction 123
Destructor 125
Deva Loka 54-56, 119, 122-123
Dharma Raj 16
Disabilities of spirits 99
Dishonesty 22
Distance 8
Divine authority 116
—ordering 59
—powers 102
—souls 104
Diwan Bahadur 128
Doctrine 60
Dogs 2
Domestic duties 80
Drafting of spirits 2
Dragging away the soul 3
Duta 2, 4-6
Duty 2, 7, 22, 29
Dying 2
—person 94

E

Elemental-s xxxvi, 34, 38, 99-101
End of the journey 12
Energiser 50
Energy xxxvi, 2, 127
English 46
Environment 75
Eternal 120
Evil consequences 101
Evolution 62
—of the soul 61
Existence of spirits xxxi, 59
Experience 61
Extraction of the soul 3

F

Fait accompli 60
Fast movement 8
Fatigue 11
Feeling-s 4
—of revenge 101
Fifth plane 46-47
Fifth-plane-spirits 92
Final destination 10
—tribunal 7
—goal 115
—Trial 107
First plane 33
—sight 97
Food 78
Force 2

Forceful extraction 2, 3
Fourth plane 19, 44
Freedom from control 39
—to move 45
Friends 97
Fruits of past life 63
Funeral ceremonies 5
Future 1

G

Gale 6
God 41, 61, 81-82, 94, 115, 119, 122, 127-128
—Himself 50
—of death 2-4, 56, 67, 104, 107, 109, 123, 125-126
—of justice 14
—of Wind 54
—like souls 54
—creations 5
Goddess of destruction 46
—of learning 42
—of Wealth 40
Good conduct 22
—deeds 21
—soul 3
Gratification 67
Great authority 105
—soul 122
—trial 13
Grief 4
Guesses about future 103
Gust of wind 7

H

Happy souls 51
Hard-hearted spirit 1
Haunting 37, 99, 100
Head of the department 23
Head-spirit 42
Health 1
Hell 17, 33
Help 101
Higher spirits 102
Hindu mythology 124
—religion 5, 59-60
Hindus xxxvii, 2, 24
His duties 123
Honest actions 21
—beliefs 21
Host of temptations and complications 62
Human actions 21

I

Idea of death 1
Identity 73
Idol xxxvii
—worship xxxvi
Ill-planned data 85
Incarnation-s 63, 68
Indian mythology 119, 121
Individual existence 107, 118
Inert soul 5
Influence-s 61, 127
—of planes 91
Inspiration xxxi, 102
Instrument-s xxxv, 30
Intelligent spirits 83
Internal management 49
Interval between successive births 28
Investigation 20
—department 20, 23

J

Journey 5, 8
Judgment 18, 20

K

Kalka 46
Karma 60-61, 116
—theory 60, 116
Kindness 5

L

Lamentations 4
Last journey 3

Layers of air 6
Leap in the dark 7
Life 1
—after death 115
—of a spirit 75
—ray 17
Living 83
—being 1
Local duties 80
Location 31
Loka-s 32-33, 41, 44-45, 106
Longevity 120
Loss of memory 53
—of touch 52
Low-bred spirits 106
Luxurious birth 64
Lurking desire 71, 83, 118

M

Materialisation xxxv, 106
Maya 43, 89, 93, 116
Machinery 104
Material advancement 116- 117
—facts 107
—instinct 71
Materialisation 37
Materialistic 71
Maya 65
Medium-s xxxii-xxxvi, 30, 43, 52, 55-56, 82, 84, 91, 94, 102, 107, 110
—speaking xxxiii
—influence 105
Mediumistic powers xxxiv
Mediumship xxxiv
Memory 110
Mental powers 99, 100, 102
Merger 17, 66, 119
Merit 5
Messenger 2, 4
—of death 3
—of yama 6
Methods of response xxxii
Mismanagement 2
Mission-s 72
—of life 60, 67
—of service 69
Moksha 17, 66-67, 118
Momentum 5
Monster of death 1
Moon 44
Mortal 1
Mournful howls 3
Mourning 4
Movement 9
Muslims 59
Murders 21
Mystery 60, 121, 127

N

Natural force xxxiv
Nerve-racking 9
Next birth 107
Noble spirit 106
Number of births 66

O

Occult 60
Orders 4
Ordinary spirits 102
Ouija board-s xxxiv-xxxvi, 110

P

Pain 2
Particular duty 77
Past birth 111
—life 62, 91, 111
Patala 13, 17, 33
—loka 33
Pavandev 54
Peep into the future 84
Perception 51
Permanent body 61
Personal attention 49
—desires 67
—equation 49
Petty investigations 81
Physical darshan 124

—end 1
—of life 1
—force 1
—senses 75, 77
Plane-s 19, 27, 31
Poignancy 4
Poverty 65
Power-s xxxiv, xxxvi, 1, 2, 123
—of gazing xxxiii
—of sight 7, 8
—of vision 7
—to call xxxi
Presiding deity 32, 50
Principal court 6
Principle of resurrection 59
Procedure at the court 20
Process of evolution 63
Production of sound 109
Progress 29
—of spirits 96
Protracted trial 19
Psychology xxxvi
Pure service 70, 129
Push 5

Q

Qualities 29

R

Ray 2
Reaping 63
Reasoning 59
Rebirth-s 5, 59, 61, 62
Record keeper 15, 23
Records 6
—of deeds 6
Region 7
Reincarnation 59, 60, 73, 117
Relatives 4, 5
Respect 5
Rest 56
Rigid tests 62
Rotation of births and deaths 61
Ruling 25

S

Salvation xxxvii, 115-116, 118-119
Saraswati devi 42
Satan 13, 101
Satya darbar 7
Satyavan 3
Savitri 3
Scope of science 2
Seances xxxi, xxxv
Second plane 38
Self 1
Self-betterment 67-68
Senses 3
Sensibilities 3
Sentiments 4
Service to the court 36
Seventh plane 54
Shadows 77
Sharp memory 100
Shelter 78
Shiva 125
Shock 4
Short lives 72
Shraddha 96
Shree Vishnu Bhagwan 50
Shree Yama Raj 48
Sixth sense 3
—plane 53
Solitary state 10
Soul-s xxxvi, 1-9, 11, 19, 27, 47, 59, 62, 90, 110-111, 127
—actions 20
—force 3
Soul's doings 6
Sound 109
Span of life 62
Spark of energy 78, 122
—of life 59
Special duties 79-80
—treatment 30
Speed 5
—ray 10, 17
Speedy transport 6

Spirit-s xxxiv-xxxvi, xxxii-xxxiv, 1-2, 5, 7, 13, 31, 39, 51, 75, 77, 82, 84-86, 91-92, 103, 105, 107, 110-111, 114
—identity 61
—communication-s xxxiii, xxxiv, 84
—communion xxxvii
—identities 72, 87
—in-charge 6-7, 9, 10, 14, 19, 24, 27
—of low order 38
—of middle class 41
—of the soul 28
—world xxxii-xxxiii, xxxvi, 5, 31, 39, 60-62, 75, 77, 117, 123
Spiritual angle of vision xxxvi
—ocean 66
Spiritualism xxxi, xxxvi, 30
Spiritually minded xxxvii
Stages or planes 31
Stagnation 59-62
Standard of justice 25
Station of life 61
Strong feelings 94
—will 3
—willed man xxxiv
Struggle 2, 4
—of death 4
Success of death 2
Suicide 3, 21
Summons 5
Supernatural force 2
—powers xxxi
Support 76
Supreme being 118-119, 124-125
—god 122, 126
Surroundings 62
Surya 46
—loka 46-48, 51-52, 79, 80, 93, 104, 118
Swarga loka 50-52
—people 51

T

Tapa 40
—loka 40, 43-44
Telepathy xxxvi
Temperament of spirits 91
Ten days' abnormal stay 4
Tender mercies 7
Terrors 11
Testing the soul 5
Tests 5
Theory of rebirth 59, 61
Third plane 40
—spirits 93
Thought-reading xxxvi
—transfer xxxvi
Toil 65
Tolerable 7
Tortuous bewilderment 2
Touch 45, 55
Transmission of news 112
Transport department 5, 7
Travel 7
Trial-s 6, 79
Troubles 53, 65
Tussle 2
Type-s of birth-s 62, 64

U

Unfulfilled desires 95
Unhappy spirits 106
Unison 28
Universe 127
Unknown region 7, 11
Unnatural death 3
Unpremeditated bad deeds 22

V

Vapour xxxv
Variation of the age 1
Vishnu 125, 127
Vision 108
Visit to the world 82
Voluntary death 4

W

Weak mediums xxxiv
Weakness 3
Westerly direction 7
Wilful wickedness 35
—wrong 22
Will-force 80
Winds 5
World 1-2, 4-5, 7
—of the Dead 44, 53
—of the living 4
Worshipper xxxvii

Y

Yama 13-14, 16-19, 20-25, 28, 42, 46, 79, 109, 123, 126-127
—in Council 15, 40
—duta 1-5
—Raj 2-3, 5, 9, 46, 48-49, 54, 61, 72, 104, 122-123, 126
Yama's court 1, 8, 12, 29, 33, 36, 126
—powers 2
—visits 46.